WHAT JESUS KNEW:

Keys to Successful Relationships

by

Ricky Thomas Gordon

WHAT JESUS KNEW:
Keys to Successful Relationships

Published by To His Glory Publishing Company, Inc.
111 Sunnydale Court
Lawrenceville, GA 30044
(770) 458-7947
www.tohisglorypublishing.com

Book is available at:
Amazon.com, BarnesandNoble.com, Borders.com

Booksamillion.com etc. and other online bookstores. This book can also be special ordered through any of your local bookstores.

To contact the author you may write to:
JesusKnew2005@aol.com

International Standard Book Number: 0-9749802-5-0

Dedication

I want to dedicate this book to the three people who have most impacted my life for good. To my mother for something she didn't do. She never asked me, "Do you want to go to church?" That was never an issue. She taught me commitment to God and to the Body of Christ. She said, "If the church is meeting, we will be there because we are members." No questions asked. That was her rule.

To my Uncle Olin who I worked with from the age of nine until I went off to college at age eighteen. Uncle Olin taught me by word and deed that you can never out give God. He gave freely and generously to all in need often at great sacrifice to himself. As I've carefully watched his life for over 40 years, I've seen God richly supply all his needs. Like Job, "The Lord blessed his latter days more than his beginning."

To my wife, Sarah, who has faithfully and unswervingly pressed me to speak the truth, love the truth and always stand-up for the truth. For over thirty-one years she has challenged and encouraged me to not just "teach" the Word but to always "live" the Word. To her, most of all, I dedicate this work.

Table of Contents

Preface

When I told a relative the title of this book, *What Jesus Knew*, he commented, "Well that just about covers everything, doesn't it?" In one sense, that is true but this work does not attempt to explain *all* that Jesus knew. The title comes from these two verses in the Gospel of John.

John 2:24-25, "But Jesus, on His part, was not entrusting Himself to them, for He knew all men,
25 and because He did not need anyone to bear witness concerning man for He Himself knew what was in man."

[Underline added by author.]

Jesus knew what was in men. He did not indiscriminately share his inner most thoughts and wisdom with all men. He was not totally open with everyone because He knew what was in the hearts of all men. He was wise in His relationships. He may have been disappointed in men but I don't think He was ever surprised at their actions.

Again and again, Jesus explained to his disciples what He knew about men and said, "These things I have spoken to you, that you may be kept from stumbling" [John 16:1]. Far too many people have been hurt and disappointed because they were so shocked by the behavior of others. Far too many

11

Christians have grown weary of the Christian life and walked away from God and the church because of their disillusionment. Jesus explained what was in man so that we would not be so surprised and discouraged by others.

David cried out to the Lord, "Give me understanding according to thy word that I may live" (Psalms 119:144,169). That has been the cry of my heart so many times. Actually, most of the time that cry has been, "Lord help me to understand this person! Why in the world did they do what they did?" I have found that if I understand before something happens, then it is much easier to deal with the effects of that action. If I become wise in the ways people relate to others, then I will not be so surprised when they relate to me in the same way.

In *What Jesus Knew,* I have condensed into Principles just some of the wisdom of the scriptures about interacting with others. It is my hope that we will become as "shrewd as serpents and innocent as doves" in all our relationships. I pray that no one will stumble from The Way of Christ because they did not know what was in man.

In all the stories I tell to illustrate the Principles, I have changed the names of everyone mentioned. The only real names used are for direct quotes and with permission.

Throughout this work, I have included almost all the scriptures that I reference in the Principles. It has been my experience that most of us will not go back later and look up the references. Therefore, I have included the verses for your ease.

Unless otherwise indicated, all scripture quotations are taken from the New American Standard Version of the Bible. Most other references will be taken from the Amplified Bible.

May God give you wisdom and understanding as you read *What Jesus Knew*. I hope that the Thirty Principles that follow will improve all your relationships and bring healing and restoration.

APPROACHING THE PRINCIPLES

"Gooney bird, gooney bird!" Pastor Kent Barber declared, watching the elderly lady at the piano looking for the sheet music that had vanished before her eyes. After the morning service the lady had picked up a sheet of music from a music stand and sat down at the piano. The guitar player, looking for his music to pack up and go home, spied it on the piano. Without even noticing the lady trying to play the piece (and, I'm kindly giving him the benefit of the doubt), the guitar player lifted the sheet music as he walked out of the sanctuary. The lady must have been looking down at the keys when the paper disappeared for she looked up in utter bewilderment at the empty space before her. She was focused only on playing the new piece. He was focused only on going home.

"Gooney birds, the body of Christ is nothing but a bunch of gooney birds," Kent mused as he walked out the door. The night before Kent had watched a special program on TV about gooney birds, another name for the black-footed albatross. The term "gooney bird" was sailor's slang for the bird and probably came from dialect "gooney fool." This was not a randomly chosen name for the birds. In the air these birds have remarkable grace and agility as they soar for hundreds of miles over the water with their seven-foot wingspan. Their problem is getting into the air.

As graceful as they are in the air, gooney birds are equally clumsy on the ground. On land that

15

magnificent wingspan is unwieldy. The special Kent had seen, showed a large group of gooney birds running down a strip of land trying to get airborne. Each bird seemed oblivious to the other as they ran en masse trying to gain enough speed to launch skyward. With hearts intent on soaring, they ran with total disregard of their fellow birds. They stumbled; they jostled; they fell. They pushed each other out of the way. They tripped each other. They stepped on each other. Each bird could only think about one thing, "I must get up into the air." Only God knows what their feelings toward their fellow gooney birds may be. If they were us, they would come forward week after week asking for inner healing!

I have often thought about Kent's description of believer's as gooney birds and have shared his story with many when teaching on relationships in the Body of Christ. It was never God's intent that we be like gooney birds. We are to be like eagles. We are to mount up with wings as eagles and soar above the storms of life. But, too often, we are like gooney birds instead. In our everyday lives we too stumble and jostle and trip and step on others. Even in our times of assembly we can become so focused on soaring into the heavenlies that we are unaware of our impact on those also attempting to get airborne. Sometimes our impact on others does more than just inconvenience or annoy them. The wound we inflict on them is deeper than a minor bruise. It may even cripple or permanently prevent another from ever reaching the sky again. Let us learn from the natural, from the Word and from both our experiences and the experiences of others. Let's all get up in the air and soar with Jesus and not leave any wounded and maimed on the airstrip below.

"What Jesus knew" was not my original choice for the title of this work. "Practical Principles Observed about People in Relationship with People," was my first choice. As I considered my reason for writing and teaching this material, I realized that more than just presenting observations from many years of experience, I wanted to prevent people from becoming disillusioned, stumbling and falling from The Way of Christ. I have had too many friends and heard too many stories of those who have been hurt and disappointed and grown weary of the Christian life mainly because they have been so shocked by the behavior of those they loved and respected. Sometimes, I have been able to help heal and restore these people to a renewed and vital walk with Christ; but, too many times, I have had poor results reaching the wounded as they cut themselves off from friends and fellowship in an attempt to prevent further pain. As a pre-emptive measure to build up the believer in an area where attacks will definitely come, I hope to add layers of protection to our Christian armor to prevent so many flaming darts from piercing and wounding our hearts.

David cried out to the Lord, "Give me understanding according to thy word that I may live" (Psalms 119:144,169). That has been the cry of my heart so many times. Actually most of the time that cry has been "Lord help me to understand this person! Why in the world did they do what they did?" I have found that if I understand before something happens, then it is much easier to deal with the effects of that action. If I become wise in the ways people relate to others, then I will not be so surprised when they relate to me in the same way.

I have been in church all my life. My mother and father were very devoted Southern Baptists. My mother first took me to church when I was three weeks old and I almost never missed any meeting our church had the nineteen years I lived at home. My father was killed in a logging accident when I was two and a half years old and my mother was seven months pregnant. Her faith never waivered and her commitment to God and His people grew stronger in those very difficult times. She taught me to be faithful no matter what happened.

During those first nineteen years I sat under many pastors and Sunday School and Training Union teachers. When I went off to university, I was introduced to the Holy Spirit and became involved with independent Charismatic churches. Since that time my wife and I have helped start two churches and worked with many others in various countries around the world. We have had the opportunity to be involved with wonderful people from a tremendous variety of racial, religious and cultural backgrounds. It has been both marvelous and painful to be in relationship with so many.

God never meant for any of us to be alone. We were made to be in relationship with God and with other people. Adam had a perfect relationship with God and he had a world full of pets, yet he had no one else like himself. Adam didn't know what he was missing. It was God who said, "It is not good for the man to be alone"(Genesis 2:18). It was God who made a helper suitable for him, someone like Adam. In the Psalms David informs us that, "God setteh the solitary [or lonely] in families" (Psalms 68:6 KJV). When estranged man is brought back into proper relationship with God through the reconciling work of Christ, he is placed into the family of God. He is given a new identity as a member of an extended family so that no matter where he goes in the world he has brothers and sisters and fathers and mothers. Jesus has promised to never leave him nor forsake him. This promise is manifested both by the Holy Spirit's indwelling presence and by relationships within the greater Family.

It is through these relationships that we are nurtured and strengthened and grow to maturity. God's design is beyond the wisdom of man. God's grace extends to all men, everywhere. His desire is that ALL be saved and come into the family. Herein we see both the goodness of God and His method of fostering growth and maturity. As a popular saying among the Baptists of my youth goes, "God catches his fish before he cleans them." God accepts anyone just as he is. He takes us "warts and all." As God is cleaning these fish, He is also using them to expose our imperfections and provoke us to greater maturity.

Someone once told me, "You can choose your friends but you can't choose your family." How true in the Family of God. God accepts people into His

Family that we would never choose to be our friends. Yet, once they are born again they are born into my family. I have no choice. I must accept and love them even though I would never choose to sit next to them on a bus or train and may not even get on an elevator with them. Now, in the twinkling of an eye, I must call this person my brother or sister.

Let me admit something here that few pastors dare admit in public. I have seen people come into a meeting and suddenly heard my emotions shout, "Oh, God I hope that person doesn't get saved here." It is not that I really don't want that person to get saved. It is just that I see so many potential problems if they get saved and become a part of OUR church. I envision years of counseling and prayer both for them and for those they will wound as they struggle to become whole. I realize this is not a cry from the Spirit of God who is drawing that person to Jesus and I must therefore reject it. I must silence my initial cry that would reject those already too wounded by rejection and listen only to the wooing words of the Holy Spirit. My goal is to feel what Jesus feels when He sees that person. My ambition is to be as loving and accepting as Jesus.

Before I moved to Japan in 1985, I was asked to share on a Sunday morning at a friend's church in a nearby city. This was a special honor for me because I had never spoken there before and I had always held this pastor in high esteem. It is always important for me to share not only from my Biblical knowledge and personal experience but also to approximate, as nearly as possible, the Lord's burden for a group.

The church leaders and I met in a small room in the back of the church to pray for the service. I prayed a simple prayer for myself, "Lord, let me feel what you feel when you look at these people."

When I prayed that prayer I really did not know what I had opened myself to receive. Although I know to be sensitive and follow the Holy Spirit, I am almost always thoroughly prepared. My bachelor's and master's degrees are in speech communication and I have taught public speaking for many years. Whenever I speak, I usually have my message well researched, organized and typed in an easy to read format. My training as both a speech teacher and a former Boy Scout always stressed, "Be prepared." That Sunday morning my notes were prepared, but my emotions were not.

I was sitting on the front row when the worship started. As the service progressed from lively praise songs to slower, more worshipful music, I was almost overwhelmed by despair and sorrow. The longer we sang the more emotional I became. I never like to lose control of my emotions and have always been suspicious of those who cry at the slightest provocation. As hard as I tried, I could not stop myself from crying. The crying rapidly advanced to a mournful weeping. People sitting behind me had no idea what was happening. What they could see was the guest speaker's shoulders bobbing up and down like a man out of control. That's what I was. I could not stop the flood of emotion.

My first thought was, "This is terrible. I'm not going to be able to say a word." My second thought

21

was, "These people don't even know me. What a terrible first impression I'm making." I am ashamed to admit that my first two thoughts were only about ME. Then I remembered my prayer, "Lord, let me feel what You feel when You look at these people." Finally, I prayed to understand the emotions that were inundating my soul.

The worship ended and my friend stood to introduce me. I think that he gave a very warm introduction although, looking at my red eyes and nose, he was a little concerned. As I stood to share, I still did not understand what had happened to me. When I turned to face the audience, I saw a young man sitting in the fourth row. I knew everything I had been feeling was for him. I knew I could not share any of my sermon until I had delivered the word of the Lord to him.

Looking at his uneasy face, the word of the Lord came. He looked me straight in the eye and I spoke. "The Lord wants you to know that He loves you very much and He has forgiven you. He wants you to forgive yourself. The Lord does not hold anything against you. He loves you. He wants you to forgive yourself just as He has."

The young man never smiled. He just nodded that he understood. The overwhelming emotions I had experienced disappeared and I was able to deliver the word I had prepared for the rest of the congregation. The young man left as soon as the meeting was over so I never got to talk to him personally.

When most people had gone home, another friend

of mine in that church asked, "Do you know who that was you had the word for at the beginning?"

"No, I don't."

"I grew up with that man. He got married a few years ago and he and his wife had a baby girl. Two weeks ago he was at home alone with the baby. He got frustrated because he was trying to work and the baby wouldn't stop crying. In his anger, he shook his baby until she stopped crying. She also stopped breathing. He killed his only child. He could come to church this morning because he's out on bail awaiting trial."

The Lord had allowed me to feel the horrible despair and hopelessness that young man was feeling. God knew and God felt his pain. When I prayed, "Lord, let me feel what you feel when you look at these people," the Lord poured some of what was in His heart into my heart. Unlike me, the Lord was not overwhelmed with the despair. He had hope for that young man and was just waiting for an available vessel to receive and deliver that hope.

Many times since that day I have prayed that simple prayer, "Lord, let me feel what You fell when You look at these people." I am still uncomfortable with some of the emotions I experience but I have learned the importance of not only receiving a word for people but also of receiving the feelings of the Lord. Romans 12:15 exhorts us to, "Rejoice with those who rejoice, and weep with those who weep." We must be willing to empathize with those we minister to. We must not misrepresent the Lord in any way. Many of us teacher types labor earnestly to accurately teach the truths of God but spend little or no time discerning the attitude in which that truth must be conveyed.

I believe the failure to accurately represent not only the truth of God but the heart of God was part of the reason Moses and Aaron were not allowed to enter the promised land. In Numbers 20, we see the people complaining once again that they have no water. Moses and Aaron seek the Lord for an answer and He responds.

Numbers 20:7-12, "And the Lord spoke to Moses, saying,
8 'Take the rod; and you and your brother Aaron assemble the congregation and speak to the rock before their eyes, that it may yield its water. You shall thus bring forth water for them out of the rock and let the congregation and their beasts drink.'
9 So Moses took the rod from before the Lord, just as He had commanded him;
10 and Moses and Aaron gathered the assembly before the rock. And he said to them, 'Listen now, you rebels; shall we bring forth water for you out of this rock?'
11 Then Moses lifted up his hand and struck the rock twice with his rod; and water came forth abundantly, and the congregation and their beasts drank.

12 But the Lord said to Moses and Aaron, 'Because you have not believed Me, to treat Me as holy in the sight of the sons of Israel, therefore you shall not bring this assembly into the land which I have given them.'"

The Lord's command was to "speak to the rock" and there is no indication that God was angry with the people. God's purpose was to meet their need. Moses fulfilled God's purpose and the people received the water they desperately needed. However, Moses was very angry with the people. He misrepresented the heart of the Father to the people. Based on his actions and words, the people would have believed that God was also angry with them. Moses was disobedient by striking the rock instead of speaking to it. I believe he was also disobedient by calling the people rebels. God judged Moses and Aaron for their actions and words and they lost the Promised Land as a result.

Even though it makes us uncomfortable to feel out of control, we must learn to open our heart to the Lord's heart, our feelings to His feelings as well as our thoughts to His thoughts. We must know the truth and share it with his attitude, whether that be compassion or righteous indignation.

In addition we need to learn from what we see and experience in our relationships with others. Proverbs 24:30-32 has become increasingly meaningful to me.

**30 "I passed by the field of the sluggard, And by the vineyard of the man lacking sense;
31 And behold, it was completely overgrown with thistles, Its surface was covered with nettles, And its stone wall was broken down.
32 When I <u>saw</u>, I <u>reflected</u> upon it; I <u>looked</u>, and <u>received instruction</u>."**
[Underline added by author.]

It is not my purpose to dwell on the problems of the sluggard, though they be many and grievous. What I wish to focus on is the observer, the one who passed by the field and stopped to learn. Verse 32 in the Amplified Bible reads "Then I beheld and considered it well; I looked and received instruction." Another translation says, "I applied my heart to understand." In other words, the writer is saying we need to be observant in our everyday lives and we need to learn from what we see. Too often we do not stop to really "see" and even when we do, we do not "consider" nor do we "receive instruction."

In **Ephesians 5:15-17 (Amplified Bible)** Paul says,

"Look carefully then how you walk! Live purposefully and worthily and accurately, not as unwise and witless, but as wise-sensible, intelligent people; Making the very most of the time buying up each opportunity--because the days are evil. Therefore do not be <u>vague and thoughtless</u>

**and foolish, but understanding and firmly
grasping what the will of the Lord is."**
[Underline added by author.]

The word translated here as "vague and thoughtless
and foolish" means to "walk without thinking,
without considering." Strong's gives the meaning
as "mindless, i.e., stupid." The wise man stops to
consider and carefully think about what he sees. The
wise man will not live his life thoughtlessly and
without purpose; but he will apply his mind and heart
to understand and receive instruction. He will be
able to make the most of every opportunity because
he will be aware of the opportunity and he will have
learned from past experience and from the mistakes
of others.

To the Romans, Paul wrote, (15:4) "For whatever
was written in earlier times was written for our
instruction, that through perseverance and the
encouragement of the Scriptures we might have
hope." To the Corinthians he said, [1 Corinthians.
10:11] "Now these things happened to them as an
example, and they were written for our instruction,
upon whom the ends of the ages have come." Clearly
it was never God's intent that we continue to be
deceived and make poor decisions when He has
given us many examples in the history of His chosen
people and that of the early church. Paul encourages
the leaders and believers in Ephesus that,

**"...we are no longer to be children,
tossed here and there by waves, and**

carried about by every wind of doctrine, by the trickery of men, by craftiness in deceitful scheming; but speaking the truth in love, we are to grow up in all aspects into Him, who is the head, even Christ."
Ephesians 4:14-15.

The writer of **Hebrews 5:14** says, " But solid food is for the mature, who because of practice have their senses trained to discern good and evil."
The Amplified Bible says, "...those whose senses and mental faculties are trained by practice to discriminate between what is morally good and noble and what is evil and contrary either to divine or human law." We are to train our minds and senses. We are to practice distinguishing evil from good. We must make a conscious effort to observe and think and discern and learn. We observe this process as Jesus trained his disciples to see what He saw.

In John 4 the disciples entered the Samaritan city of Sychar with Jesus. However, they were looking at the city and the situation very differently from Jesus. They were hungry men looking for food. Jesus saw a thirsty woman in need of living water. They saw only Samaritans, whom "the Jews have nothing to do with " (v. 9). Jesus saw a city ripe for the harvest. The disciples found bread for the body. Jesus found a woman and an entire city ready to eat the bread of life and drink the living water that would make them part of His Body. Jesus' conversation with his disciples (after the woman at the well had departed to tell everyone about the great prophet she had met) reveals some of the differences in the way Jesus viewed the situation and the way the disciples did.

> **John 4:31-38, "In the meanwhile the disciples were requesting Him, saying, 'Rabbi, eat.'**
> **32 But He said to them, 'I have food to eat that you do not know about.'**
> **33 The disciples therefore were saying to one another, "No one brought Him anything to eat, did he?'**
> **34 Jesus said to them, 'My food is to do the will of Him who sent Me, and to accomplish His work.**
> **35 "Do you not say, 'There are yet four months, and then comes the harvest'? Behold, I say to you, lift up your eyes, and look on the fields, that they are white for harvest.**
> **36 "Already he who reaps is receiving wages, and is gathering fruit for life eternal; that he who sows and he who reaps may rejoice together.**
> **37 "For in this case the saying is true, 'One sows, and another reaps.'**
> **38 "I sent you to reap that for which you have not labored; others have labored, and you have entered into their labor."**

The disciples saw the same people, place and

situation as Jesus but they did not really see the way Jesus saw. Jesus was training them to see beyond the natural, beyond the outward appearance, and see as God sees. This was part of their practice to train both their natural and spiritual senses.

In Matthew we are allowed to read a brief conversation Jesus had with a group of religious leaders.

Matthew 16:1-3, "And the Pharisees and Sadducees came up, and testing Him asked Him to show them a sign from heaven.
2 But He answered and said to them, When it is evening, you say, 'It will be fair weather, for the sky is red.'
3 And in the morning, 'There will be a storm today, for the sky is red and threatening.' Do you know how to discern the appearance of the sky, but cannot discern the signs of the times? ' "

Jesus rebuked the leaders of Israel as men who could discern the sky and the weather but could not discern the times in which they lived. People may train their natural senses to discern the sky and learn from the warning signs in nature, yet remain oblivious to far more important and serious signs.

Frequently in scripture we are warned to "be not deceived." [I Corinthians 6:9; 15:33; Gal. 6:7; James 1:16, etc.] Jesus begins his discussion of end time events by saying in Matthew 24:4 (RSV), "do not be led astray." Particularly in these last days we need to train our senses to discern. We cannot afford to mindlessly and thoughtlessly walk through the days of our lives lest, by our complacency, we be led astray. Proverbs 1:32 says, "For the waywardness of the naive shall kill them, And the complacency of fools shall destroy them." Complacency is defined here as "self-satisfaction accompanied by an unawareness of real danger or need." Complacency is a characteristic of fools, not of Christians. Complacency will destroy us. We are not those who are destined for destruction but we are destined for life, and life more abundantly both now and in eternity. Therefore complacency is not to be part of our nature.

A good example of complacency was the church at Laodicea described in Revelations chapter three.

Revelations 3:15-20, "I know your deeds, that you are neither cold nor hot; I would that you were cold or hot.
16 So because you are lukewarm, and neither hot nor cold, I will spit you out of My mouth.
17 Because you say, 'I am rich, and have become wealthy, and have need of nothing,' and you do not know that you are wretched and miserable and poor and blind and naked,
18 I advise you to buy from Me gold refined by fire, that you may become rich, and white garments, that you may clothe yourself, and that the shame of

**your nakedness may not be revealed;
and eye salve to anoint your eyes, that
you may see.**
**19 Those whom I love, I reprove and
discipline; be zealous therefore, and
repent.**
**20 Behold, I stand at the door and
knock; if anyone hears My voice and
opens the door, I will come in to him,
and will dine with him, and he with
Me. "**

The Laodicean Christians believed they were fine.
They honestly thought they were "wealthy and [had]
need of nothing." Yet Christ looked at them and
said they were in great need and in danger of being
cast out. Literally in verse 16, it says "I will **vomit**
you out of my mouth." That is some very strong
language for the Lord of all creation to say to a
church!

Most evangelicals use verse 20 when witnessing
to unbelievers but that verse is talking to a church!
Jesus is saying to these complacent church people,
"I am on the outside knocking. Open the door and
let me in." A church without Jesus inside isn't really
a church. It is just a group of religious people
practicing dead traditions.

Wayne Cordeiro of Hope Chapel in Hawaii once
told this story to illustrate how complacency leads to
ruin. In this case, it was economic ruin.

"Let me tell you a story. It was in the

1940's that Swiss watches were the most prestigious and best quality in the world--Swiss watches. Eighty percent of the world's watches were made in Switzerland. They had employed over 80,000 people in watch factories—in Switzerland. 80,000. In the late 50's a digital watch was presented to the leaders of this Swiss watch company. The developer said, 'Here, this is a digital watch. We'd like to present it to you.' The makers at the Swiss watch company laughed. They said, 'How stupid you are. You think we're going to change? We've got the world market.' And they rejected the idea. You know why? Because they were fine. They were fine people. 'We're fine.' The person who developed the digital watch turned around and offered it to the second one in line, Seiko of Japan. They took it.

In the 40's a Swiss watch company employed over 80,000 people. Now they employ under 10,000. In 1940, 80% of the watches were made in Switzerland. Today, 80% are made in Japan. Less than 8% are made in Switzerland. Why? This is what happens to people who choose to be, 'We're fine. I don't need to change. We got it. We got the tiger by the tail. I'm fine.' And the graph begins to spiral downwards."

As part of their training Jesus taught the disciples what to look for in the coming days. One reason Jesus told them in advance was to confirm his claim to be God's son.

John 13:18-19, "I do not speak of all of you. I know the ones I have chosen; but it is that the Scripture may be fulfilled, He who eats My bread has lifted up his heel against Me.
19 From now on I am telling you before it comes to pass, so that when it does occur, you may believe that I am He. "
[Underline added by author.]

In effect, Jesus is saying that when these things happen, "when I am betrayed, remember I told you this would happen. When you remember, let this confirm to you that I am the Christ. Don't get discouraged and run away. Let this strengthen your belief in Me." Likewise when we experience these types of problems let this confirm to us the validity and reliability of God's Word.

Another reason Jesus warned his disciples about what was going to happen and how people would treat them was so that they would not be shocked and stumble.

John 16:1-4 "These things I have spoken to you, that you may be kept from stumbling.
2 They will make you outcasts from the

synagogue, but an hour is coming for everyone who kills you to think that he is offering service to God.
3 And these things they will do, because they have not known the Father, or Me.
4 <u>But these things I have spoken to you, that when their hour comes, you may remember that I told you of them</u>. And these things I did not say to you at the beginning, because I was with you. "
[Underline added by author.]

Jesus was concerned about the 12 men who had followed Him most closely, who had witnessed first-hand and had even participated in some of his most remarkable miracles. He did not want them to be shocked or shaken by what would happen. He was concerned that they would be tempted to stumble and perhaps even give up. He warned them ahead of time and instructed them when it happened, "remember that I told you of them."

Paul also warned the Ephesian elders when he summoned them at Miletus. In Acts 20:17-38, we have Paul's final words to the leaders of the church. Pay close attention to verses 28-32.

Acts 20:28-32, "Be on guard for yourselves and for all the flock, among which the Holy Spirit has made you overseers, to shepherd the church of God which He purchased with His own blood.

29 I know that after my departure savage wolves will come in among you, not sparing the flock;

30 and from among your own selves men will arise, speaking perverse things, to draw away the disciples after them.

31 Therefore be on the alert, remembering that night and day for a period of three years I did not cease to admonish each one with tears.

32 And now I commend you to God and to the word of His grace, which is able to build you up and to give you the inheritance among all those who are sanctified. "

Paul does three things:

1) He instructs them to take heed, be alert, take care and be on guard. In other words, be observant, pay attention, stop and think. This is not only for their benefit but also for the benefit of those God has given them to watch over.
2) He tells them to watch for certain types of people. Not everyone among you is good and righteous. Know and understand so that you will not be deceived or that those under your care will not be led astray.
3) He commends/commits them to God's care and grace. This is a reassurance that no matter what happens God and His grace are sufficient.

Paul gave advance warning to the believers about the second coming of Christ and the coming of the Antichrist so that they would not be shocked and shaken when it did happen.

> **2 Thessalonians 2:1-5, "Now we request you, brethren, with regard to the coming of our Lord Jesus Christ, and our gathering together to Him,** <u>**2 that you may not be quickly shaken from your composure or be disturbed**</u> **either by a spirit or a message or a letter as if from us, to the effect that the day of the Lord has come. 3 Let no one in any way deceive you, for it will not come unless the apostasy comes first, and the man of lawlessness is revealed, the son of destruction, 4 who opposes and exalts himself above every so-called god or object of worship, so that he takes his seat in the temple of God, displaying himself as being God.** <u>**5 Do you not remember that while I was still with you, I was telling you these things?**</u> **"**

[Underline added by author.]

Paul uses almost the same words as Jesus. He is concerned that they may not "be quickly shaken" and he warns them to remember that he had told them in advance what would happen.

Both Jesus and Paul warned them of the most devastating thing that could happen to them--betrayal by those closest to them. Jesus warned in Matthew10:21 that, "...Brother will deliver up brother to death, and a father his child; and children will rise up against parents, and cause them to be put to death." Paul said, "From among your own selves men will arise, speaking perverse things, to draw away the disciples after them." It is not strangers who cause most believers to be quickly shaken, disturbed and stumble. It is when those closest to us, those we least expect, turn against us or turn aside from the truth.

David eloquently vented his emotions when betrayed by an intimate friend:

**Psalms 55:12-14, "For it is not an enemy who reproaches me, Then I could bear it; Nor is it one who hates me who has exalted himself against me, Then I could hide myself from him.
13 But it is you, a man my equal, My companion and my familiar friend.
14 We who had sweet fellowship together, Walked in the house of God in the throng. "**

If an enemy turns against us and seeks to destroy our reputation and/or our very life, we can understand that and we can find some way to deal with the injury. But we can hardly bear it when our close friend, our mate, our fellow believer or even our pastor seeks to devastate us. As a result, many are shaken and stumble.

As believers and leaders we have a responsibility to be wise and to be prepared. We are to follow the almost contradictory commandment of Christ.

Matthew 10:16, "Behold, I send you out as sheep in the midst of wolves; therefore be shrewd as serpents, and innocent as doves. "

How can we be as "shrewd as serpents" and yet remain as "innocent as doves?" How can we be on guard against deceivers and yet remain kind and loving to all? How do we avoid becoming as cynical as many we are called to heal who have been hurt and wounded again and again and again? We know we must heed the warning to "Watch over your heart with all diligence, For from it flow the springs of life" (Proverbs 4:23). Yet, how do we watch over or guard our hearts and, at the same time, keep our hearts open to those God places in our lives?

I remember the frustration I felt in church when I was young. My teachers would say, "You are supposed to be like Jesus." Then they would hastily add, "But, of course, you can never be just like Jesus." Others would read the scriptures that said, "Be thou holy as I am holy," and tell us that we were supposed to be "holy." This was almost always followed by the disclaimer, "But, of course, Jesus is the only one who was holy." I couldn't understand why God was always telling us to do things He knew we couldn't do. It was only after I had spent almost twenty years of my life in church that I heard about the work and power of the Holy Spirit that would enable us to be and do all that the Bible said. So I believe it is possible to "be shrewd as serpents, and innocent as doves."

Jesus prayed for us that we would be able to walk in the world and yet not be of the world. He is still living to always intercede on our behalf. Jesus is standing for us that we will be able to love as He loved, yet knowing all the while that each of us has one or more Judas' to face in our lives.

For myself, I have always taken comfort in recognizing that I was warned beforehand that what had happened to me was a possibility and that there was nothing happening to me that had not already happened to some other believer before or that was possibly happening to some other believer at this very moment.

1 Peter 5:8-10, "Be of sober spirit, be on the alert. Your adversary, the devil, prowls about like a roaring lion, seeking someone to devour.
9 But resist him, firm in your faith, <u>knowing that the same experiences of suffering are being accomplished by your brethren who are in the world.</u>
10 And after you have suffered for

a little while, the God of all grace, who called you to His eternal glory in Christ, will Himself perfect, confirm, strengthen and establish you. "
V. 9, Amplified Bible, "...knowing that the same (identical) sufferings are appointed to your brotherhood (the whole body of Christians) throughout the world. "
[Underline added by author.]

1 Corinthians 10:13, "No temptation has overtaken you but such as is common to man; and God is faithful, who will not allow you to be tempted beyond what you are able, but with the temptation will provide the way of escape also, that you may be able to endure it."

God is faithful! God's grace is sufficient for all our needs. We can trust Him to help us in all our relationships. We can be wise and innocent at the same time.

Most of the principles that follow this introduction were first taught at Good Samaritan Fellowship Bible School in Madurai, south India to a group of aspiring young pastors. I have since added to those initial principles and sought to explain them more clearly. Looking back over that first teaching I felt that, overall, I had presented the information in a more negative way than I wanted. I do not want to create a suspicious attitude in those who read these words and I do not want to add to the cynicism that is already too prevalent in battle weary soldiers.

What I desire is to help all of us identify patterns of behavior, first in ourselves and then in others, that can be corrected before serious problems arise. We live in a fallen world and everyone of us, as long as we are breathing, will be tempted to yield to sin. Our greatest concern must be those sins that so easily entangle us (Hebrews 12:1), those which we too often repeat. Some of these are our own, individualized sins, and others are those that have been passed down from generation to generation. Some are taught patterns of sin and others are "family demons" handed down. Let me give a few examples.

First, consider Abraham and Isaac. On two different occasions Abraham feared for his life and told a half truth about his wife, Sarah. In Genesis 12:10-20 Abraham goes to Egypt but fears that he will be killed so that the Egyptians can have his beautiful wife. He tells Sarah to lie by saying she is his sister. Pharaoh takes her into his household and treats Abraham very nicely because of his beautiful sister. God rescues Sarah by sending plagues on Pharaoh's household until he realizes what Abraham has done.

Years later Abraham takes his family to Gerar (Genesis 20:1-18) and once again fears he will be killed because of his beautiful wife. King Abimelech takes Sarah into his household until God appears to him in a dream and says, "Behold, you

are a dead man, because of the woman whom you
have taken; for she is a man's wife." (v. 3) Again,
God rescues Sarah, the obedient wife.

Both these events happened before Isaac was
born (Genesis 21:1-3). Isaac did not personally
witness his father do these things; yet years later,
when he has a wife, Rebekah, he repeats the sin of
his father. Isaac, too, goes to Gerar due to a famine
(Genesis 26:6-11). He too fears for his life because
of his beautiful wife and lies that she is his sister.
King Abimelech looked out a window one day and
saw Isaac "fondling" (RSV) Rebekah and confronts
Isaac. Abimelech is so upset he warns all the people
that "Whoever touches this man or his wife shall
be put to death." (v. 11). We see a pattern of sin
repeated in the life of the son.

By the third generation, the grandson is even
named "deceiver." The deceiver, Jacob, also
continues to lie as he pretends to be his elder
brother, Esau. Lying seems to run in the family.

Another example of a pattern of sin being
repeated in a family is seen in David. David had
a weakness for the ladies. God's design, regardless
of what kings and cultures advocate, is one husband
having one wife. God did not give Adam a harem.
He created "a" helper, not helpers, suitable for
Adam. David had 7 wives, but his greatest sin was
committing adultery with Bathsheba, lying about it
and having her husband killed.

This weakness in the father is greatly magnified
in his son, Solomon. Solomon had 700 wives and
300 concubines (I Kings 11:1-4). Most of these

were women from countries that God had forbidden the people of Israel to marry. The scripture tells us that when Solomon was old these women turned his heart away from the living God to other gods.

Tradition also tells that when the queen of Sheba returned home after visiting Solomon she was pregnant with his child. Both modern Ethiopia and Yemen claim to have been ruled by the Queen of Sheba. "The Ethiopian story continues to say that the Queen returned to her homeland and gave birth to a son, Menelek. When Menelek became of age (21) he went to visit his father, Solomon. Solomon re-named Menelek, David II after Solomon's father, and anointed him King of Zion." (from "The Story of the Queen of Sheba" By Miri Hunte Haruach, at: *http://www.goddessaltar.com/ sheba_the_legend.htm The Story)* "The Ethiopian epic seems to have been compiled and recorded in writing during the 13th century, but its origin is difficult to determine. It is certainly true that from the restoration of the Solomonic Dynasty around 1270 until the death of the last emperor, Haile Selassie I, in 1975, the emperors of Ethiopia claimed descent from Solomon and the Queen of Sheba. The claim was even part of the constitution proclaimed by Selassie in 1955." ("Queen of Sheba, *http://www.africana.com/tt_261.htm).*

David's weakness was not only passed on to his son but was extended to an extreme proportion that led to devastating consequences. It behooves us to identify similar patterns in our own families so that they may not be passed on to the next generation.

In my own family there was a clearly identifiable pattern of fear passed down for at least four generations. When the Lord started the process of deliverance and healing from the ravages of fear in my life, I researched my family history for answers. I knew my mother had many fears that had bound her from her youth. She had a terrible fear of snakes and a strong fear of water, mainly the fear of drowning. Most of my youth she lived in fear that someone would come into our house and harm us. This fear manifested itself in what I considered to be a strange ritual. Whenever we returned home at night, my mother would carefully lock the door. Then we had to go through the house looking under beds and inside closets to see if anyone was hiding there. This never made sense to me. What would we do if we found someone? We had already locked ourselves in with them!

In conversations with my mother I learned that her mother had had a terrible fear of storms. My mother remembered that as a child her mother would gather all the children into the bed with her whenever a storm came. My grandmother would hold all her children tightly and shake in fear until the storm was over. My mother remembers her mother talking about how afraid her own mother (my great grandmother) had been. We clearly identified four generations of fear.

In my own family I feel that the pattern of fear was both a "family demon" passed down and a "learned response" to certain events. There was a need to cast out the family demon and to renew my mind according to God's Word. God set me free and worked backwards to help my mother. She never gained total victory before her death but she lived far more victoriously her latter years than she did when I was growing up.

When my first child was born, we quickly saw the same weakness appear in his personality. My son, Chris, had an unnatural fear of anyone wearing any kind of mask. I know that God had determined to end this pattern of fear with my generation and had prepared me to help in ways my mother never knew. We prayed for Chris frequently and taught him how to stand against fear by relying on

God's Word. One of the first scriptures he learned was "what time I am afraid, I will trust in Thee" (Psalms 56:3 KJV). Within a few years he had overcome his fears. Later, he was so adventuresome we almost wished he was afraid of something.

The "practical principles observed about people in relationship with people" that follow are guidelines, not absolutes. There are exceptions to almost every rule and principle that regards people. Only the Word of God has absolute truth and as David so aptly put it, "The sum of thy word is truth" [Psalms 119:160]. All of God's word taken together is absolute truth. Therefore, any principles set forth by man, no matter how wise that man, must always be yielded to the Holy Spirit for Him to teach and apply to our lives. It is my prayer that as you continue to read you may keep your eyes, ears and hearts open to THE teacher and that He may apply what you need to your relationships. May we be as magnanimous as Christ, forgiving every offense as quickly as possible. And, as we soar in the heavenlies with Christ, let go of everything that happened to us on the ground and think only of the joy we know in His presence.

Principle 1:

People are important to God and are therefore important to me!

First, and foremost, people were important enough for Jesus to abandon heaven and His exalted position, be born in a stable, live and suffer among us, and die a horrible death on the cross. We are created in the image of God and He gave the best that He had to redeem us and bring us back into relationship with Him. He plans for people to spend eternity with Him. Therefore, no matter how people may treat us, we must always remember how important we all are to God. What God treasures, we must treasure. What God loves, we must love. And, He loves and treasures people.

Never lose site of this one point--just one person, no matter who or where they are, is of infinite value and concern to God. Those who seek Him will find him, even if he has to send one of his servants half way around the world just to tell that person.

Another important point is that time and money do not mean the same to God as they do to us. Billy Graham was once criticized by someone for spending a large sum of money on one crusade. When pressed to justify the expenditure, Mr. Graham responded with this query. "If you can tell me how much YOUR soul is worth, I'll tell you how much I should spend on a crusade." Mr. Graham did not have to justify his crusade expenses for the man could not put a price on his OWN soul. The only price God ever put on a soul was the price of His Son. No money in all the world can pay for that.

My second trip to India (1982) I visited Pastor Abraham in Ajmer, a major city in the desert state of Rajasthan. One morning brother Abraham awakened me early and said we had to leave for the bus very soon. He felt we needed to go farther into Rajasthan to encourage a brother pioneering a church. We hastily ate breakfast and walked to the local bus station. I was still rather sleepy; the temperature was rising; and, the bus was noisy and bumpy as usual. So, we didn't talk much on the three-hour ride.

Although brother Samuel did not know we were coming, he was near the bus station when we arrived. He was overjoyed to see his old friend and fellow pioneer. Brother Samuel was very excited to see me and eagerly escorted us to his house. He said nothing about the morning's events or even how the church planting was going.

When we arrived at his home, his wife politely greeted us and hurriedly began preparing a meal for her unexpected guests. She scurried in and out of the room as she prepared everything. In contrast to her husband who never stopped grinning, she never smiled. I didn't think anything about this because it is not that unusual in India, particularly when the woman can't communicate in English and is left out of the conversation among the men.

We were served a wonderful meal. It was especially wonderful since nothing was too hot or spicy for me to eat. As is the custom, the women serve the men first and only after they have eaten do the women sit to eat. When brother Samuel's wife cleared the last dish from the table she returned to the room where we were conversing. With a very serious and stern looking face she stood in front of me and spoke. Her husband interpreted these words, "I have given you natural food to eat. Now you give me spiritual food. What does the Lord have to say to me?"

I was completely caught off guard. The temperature in the room had risen with the noon day sun. I was full and ready to take a nap and I hadn't done anything spiritual all morning. But I knew this woman was very, very earnest in her request.

While we shuffled the furniture to make room to accommodate everyone in a more relaxed way, I prayed fervently under my breath for God to give me something quickly. One passage of scripture came to mind so I asked her husband to read these words to her from her Bible.

Malachi 3:13-18, "Your words have been arrogant against Me, says the Lord. Yet you say, 'What have we spoken against Thee?'
14 You have said, 'It is vain to serve God; and what profit is it that we have kept His charge, and that we have walked in mourning before the Lord of hosts?
15 So now we call the arrogant blessed; not only are the doers of wickedness built up, but they also test God and escape.'

16 Then those who feared the Lord spoke to one another, and the Lord gave attention and heard it, and a book of remembrance was written before Him for those who fear the Lord and who esteem His name.

17 And they will be Mine, says the Lord of hosts, on the day that I prepare My own possession, and I will spare them as a man spares his own son who serves him.

18 So you will again distinguish between the righteous and the wicked, between one who serves God and one who does not serve Him."

These seemed like harsh words for me, a stranger, to tell this woman who had just fed me lunch. It was all I had received so it was all I could give. She made no comment. I proceeded in faith (which was getting harder and harder to do since she still had not changed her stony countenance). I told her I felt she had said harsh words complaining against the Lord and that he wanted her to know he had not forgotten her nor her family. I encouraged her that God did, indeed, see her and all her suffering and that her name and deeds were written in a book of remembrance. I said that one day the time would come when she would be honored above the wicked and it would be proven that she was from God. I further felt that God was preparing a crown and that she would be a jewel in His crown.

She stood there in silence. I really didn't know

what to do now. So, I did what most pastors do when they don't know what to say or do. I said, "Let's pray." Now prayer is always good, but let's be honest. Anyone who's been a Christian, especially a leader, for some time can pray very long general prayers as they stall for time to think. This is even easier when you've got an interpreter that slows down the process.

When I ran out of general requests and blessings, I laid my hands on her head and began to pray in tongues. She began to cry. The more I prayed in tongues the more she wept, until she was moaning and sobbing. My first thought was, "Oh, Lord, what am I doing to this poor woman!" It became clear that the Holy Spirit was ministering to her and breaking down barriers inside her. Finally, she broke and wept tears of joy mingled with tears of repentance. Her husband was also now crying and rejoicing. Brother Abraham and I did not know what was going on and had to wait until they got control of themselves to tell us. This was their story.

The reason Brother Samuel was near the bus station when we arrived was because he had left his home in utter despair that morning. Their church planting looked like it was going nowhere. They were the only Christians in the city. Their children were teased and taunted by other children and even had stones thrown at them as they walked along the street. The local school officials were talking about refusing entry to their children because they were Christians. Everyone seemed blessed and prosperous around them while they felt rejected and battered.

That morning his wife came to a breaking point. She was angry with God for what was happening to her and her children. Her husband could not give her any satisfactory answers. When Brother Samuel left the house, his wife was on the floor crying out to God, "My God, my God, why have you forsaken us?" Both felt badly beaten and defeated and were ready to give up and move away.

Thanks to the sensitivity of Brother Abraham and the scripture and words provided by the Holy Spirit, this couple was restored, strengthened and encouraged that they were of great value to God. I was in awe of God's ways. I genuinely felt this one event was my main reason for going to India that summer. If that was all that I accomplished, then that trip was a complete success. It did not matter how far I had to travel, how much money I spent or how tired I got. God would go to any length to answer the cry of a desperate saint about to be defeated. They were that important to Him.

There is one more miracle to this story. One year later I was back in India. I boarded a crowded train in Madurai, twelve hundred miles (1,935 km) from where I had met brother and sister Samuel. I stepped on the train and heard someone call my name. It was brother Samuel and his happy wife. They had been on a visit to see family and were on their way home. It was wonderful to hear their story of how God had broken through in their town with many salvations. A good church had been planted and was growing, all by God's great grace. This time Samuel's wife smiled as much as he did. Now what's the probability of one American, stepping on a train in a south Indian city one year later, and meeting two out of almost one billion Indians? Astronomical! With God all things are possible.

Principle 2:

You really don't know what is inside people.

We don't know the good or the evil that is deep inside people. Jesus knows. The Holy Spirit knows. But you don't know. Good things, bad things, talents, abilities, hurts, memories, deeds, abortions, divorces, substance abuse, etc. lie hidden beneath the surface of outward appearance. But you can be sure that what is inside will come out at some point. The Word is clear about this. Given enough time and interaction, the inner truth will be revealed. Thousands of years before Christ, God spoke through Moses a warning to His newly chosen people.

Numbers 32:23, "... be sure your sin will find you out. "

This verse has particular significance in my personal history. My mother repeated "...be sure your sins will find you out" again and again to me. I was a lot more mischievous than my younger brother so this seemed to be her favorite verse for her first born. She almost always said that part of the verse as I was going out with the guys on Friday or Saturday night. It was a warning which usually went like this, "Be good. I won't be there to see what you do but God sees everything and He'll let me know. Remember, 'be sure your sins will find you out.'"

In my small hometown of Abbeville, Alabama, population 3,000, the most evil place in town was

Lloyd's Pool Hall. It was the only place that sold
beer then and it was rumored that people actually
gambled there. My mother repeatedly warned me
not to go in there. She often repeated the story about
my father who had borrowed money from the owner
of the pool hall for the down payment on our home.
My father refused to go into the pool hall to make his
monthly payments because he didn't want anyone
to see him going in and out and think that he was
drinking or gambling. Then, she quoted her second
favorite verse for me, "A good name is to be more
desired than great riches, Favor is better than silver
and gold" [Proverbs 22:1].

With all this warning, Lloyd's Pool Hall had a
particular fascination for me. Many of my friends
regularly sneaked in to play pool. Finally, one
Saturday night my curiosity got the better of me. I
parked my car far down the street from the pool hall.
Searching the empty street very carefully, I leapt out
of my car and ran to the door of the pool hall, making
one last look around to be sure no one could see me.
I must admit I was so nervous inside the pool hall I
really couldn't enjoy my first visit to Abbeville's great
den of iniquity. After about 30 minutes I slipped out the
front door and ran down the street to my parked car. I
was sure no one had seen me.

I drove around for a few minutes before heading
home. When I opened the back door and walked in
my mother was standing there waiting. "And where
have you been tonight, young man?" To this day,
I still don't know who called my mother and told
her they had seen me in the pool hall. No one could

have been more careful than I. I have no memory of what my mother said or what my punishment was. I only know that the fear of God, and my mother, was indelibly marked on my soul that night. Years later when I went away to college, that lesson kept me from yielding to many available temptations. More than once I walked away from sin because I was convinced that whatever I did, even far away from home, would be revealed to my mother later.

Jesus made it clear that what is in the heart will come out.

Matthew 12:34-35, "You brood of vipers, how can you, being evil, speak what is good? <u>For the mouth speaks out of that which fills the heart.</u>
35 "The good man out of his good treasure brings forth what is good; and the evil man out of his evil treasure brings forth what is evil."
[Underline added by author.]

Luke 6:45,"The good man out of the good treasure of his heart brings forth what is good; and the evil man out of the evil treasure brings forth what is evil; <u>for his mouth speaks from that which fills his heart.</u> " *[Underline added by author.]*

During my third year as a leader in a local church, I worked with an older man whose wife had a very acerbic tongue. Frequently he had to explain to those she had hurt. I tried to talk to the brother about his wife and that this happened too often to just be occasional verbal slips. His reply was, "I know she says some bad things but her heart is good." Almost without thinking I shot back, "but the Bible says that 'out of the abundance of the heart the mouth speaketh.'" I'm not sure it was the wisest thing for me to blurt out, especially so directly. He and his wife left the church not too long after that.

His explanation represents a common myth perpetrated in the world. That myth is "he may do bad things but he really has good intentions." TV and movies always portray the prostitute with "the heart of gold" or the thief who is really, deep down, a very compassionate and generous guy. That sounds good to many but the Word is quite clear. Whatever fills the heart is going to come out. Yes, evil people are tempted to do good and they sometimes yield to that temptation; but, they are still evil. Born again, Bible believing Christians are tempted to do evil and sometimes yield to that temptation. However, we are not to continue in that sin and we are to make an effort to change our behavior to conform to the image of Christ.

Ideally, we will be in a loving, caring church involved with people to the point that we can openly reveal our problems and seek help. We know that many of us keep things hidden until they are revealed through our words or actions. Until then, many around us do not know. It reminds me of the old radio program, "The Shadow." As part of the prologue to each program you would hear, "Who knows what evil lurks in the hearts of men? The Shadow knows." That was a warning to strike fear in the hearts of evil doers.

Far more important than "The Shadow" knowing what is in our hearts, Jesus and the Holy Spirit know what is in the hearts of men. The only way we can really know (before something happens) is if the Holy Spirit reveals it to us.

John 2:23-25, "Now when He was in Jerusalem at the Passover, during the feast, many believed in His name, beholding His signs which He was doing.
24 But Jesus, on His part, was not entrusting Himself to them, for <u>He knew all men,</u>
25 and because He did not need anyone to bear witness concerning man for <u>He Himself knew what was in man.</u>"
[Underline added by author.]

Romans 8:26-27, "And in the same way the Spirit also helps our weakness; for we do not know how to pray as we should, but the Spirit Himself intercedes for us with groanings too deep for words;
27 and He who searches the hearts knows what the mind of the Spirit is,

because He intercedes for the saints according to the will of God."

1 Corinthians 2:10-13, "For to us God revealed them through the Spirit; for the Spirit searches all things, even the depths of God.
11 For who among men knows the thoughts of a man except the spirit of the man, which is in him? Even so the thoughts of God no one knows except the Spirit of God.
12 Now we have received, not the spirit of the world, but the Spirit who is from God, that we might know the things freely given to us by God,
13 which things we also speak, not in words taught by human wisdom, but in those taught by the Spirit, combining spiritual thoughts with spiritual words."

Let me share a few examples of how God can help his people by revealing hidden things. During the first few years my wife and I were involved in ministry, we became great friends with Carl and Sheena. As our church grew and became more involved in the lives of families, we got to know Carl's mother and his older sister, Heather. The Holy Spirit was moving through Carl to reach back into the family history and reveal and redeem many unpleasant events.

Heather lived in another state not too far from us. She and her husband were actively involved in a growing Charismatic church. The more involved they became the more the sister's personal problems began to surface. No matter how hard she tried, she just could not feel at home in the church. Intellectually, she knew everything was all right. As far as she could tell, she loved everyone and wanted to be with them; but, when she was at church, she always felt uncomfortable. She just felt like she did not fit.

Heather and her husband began to seek the Lord for an answer. The only verse she received was in Deuteronomy in a passage talking about the curse that comes upon illegitimate children. The verse says, "No one of illegitimate birth shall enter the assembly of the Lord; none of his descendants, even to the tenth generation, shall enter the assembly of the Lord" [Deuteronomy 23:2]. She did not see how this verse could apply to her because she knew when her parents wedding anniversary was and she knew her birth date. She was born within the first year but after her parents had been married over 9 months. This one verse was all the information she felt God had given her.

Summoning her courage, she visited her mother and told what the Lord had shown her. To her mother's credit, she told her daughter the truth. Her mother had been pregnant when she married and her parents had lied to her about their wedding date all these years. What God had revealed was true. Through prayer the curse of illegitimacy was broken so that this renewed young woman could experience the full acceptance Christ had won for her at the cross.

Let me share another example. Some years ago

we had special meetings in our church in Japan with a prophet from America. One of our church members brought her skeptical husband to an evening meeting. Before he came up, the man asked the Lord to show him He was real. As the prophet prayed for the couple he shared what he was seeing. The prophet described a child he saw separated from the rest of the family. The husband said there was nothing like that. The wife turned white. Then, almost trembling, she confessed that she had gotten pregnant some years after her other children were already teenagers. Because they were embarrassed about the pregnancy, she had an abortion. But, she had never told anyone. God confirmed himself to this man.

In 1 Corinthians 2:9-10, Paul wrote,

9 "But just as it is written, Things which eye has not seen and ear has not heard, And which have not entered the heart of man, All that God has prepared for those who love Him.
10 For to us God revealed them through the Spirit; for the Spirit searches all things, even the depths of God."

Paul's emphasis is that God has so much more prepared for us than we know, things we have not even dreamed about yet. But God does not want to keep these things hidden from us. He has made a way to reveal them to us through the Holy Spirit.

Paul wrote similar words of encouragement to the church in Ephesus.

Ephesians 3:20-21, "Now to Him who is able to do exceeding abundantly beyond all that we ask or think, according to the power that works within us,
21 to Him be the glory in the church and in Christ Jesus to all generations forever and ever. Amen."

God is able to do far beyond all that we can ask or think. Some people have no trouble making their many requests known to God. Some of us big dreamers have well developed imaginations, yet God is able to do exceeding abundantly more than what we can imagine or ask. God exceeds all our mental powers.

Earlier in Ephesians 2:10 Paul had informed them that "...We are His workmanship, created in Christ Jesus for good works, which God prepared beforehand, that we should walk in them." I believe Paul was inspiring them to find out what good works God had already prepared for them to do and to start doing those things. His later admonition in 3:20 was to reach beyond what they already knew and press on to even greater works.

One of my favorite real-life stories is about Mrs. Anna Mary Robertson Moses. Anna was born in 1860 in the hills of Washington County in upper New York State. She married young and spent most of her life helping her husband on the farm and raising their children. When she was in her seventies she developed arthritis in her hands and visited the local doctor complaining that she had trouble sewing. He suggested she try something else to keep her fingers from stiffening. Someone suggested she take up painting. Anna had never had the time or money for such frivolous indulgences. Someone donated her first art supplies so she tried painting, just to keep her fingers limber.

The local drugstore owner liked her colors and asked if he could display her work in his drugstore window. New York art collector Louis Calder passed through town and saw the drugstore display. He bought some of the paintings and took them back to New York City. The year she turned 79, three of her paintings were exhibited in the Museum of Modern Art in New York City. The following year the Gallerie Saint Étienne in New York City presented her first solo show. Her career was launched.

Anna, better known as Grandma Moses, who had no formal training (virtually of any kind) was celebrated as one of America's most original artists. She had never dreamed nor had it entered into her mind the talent that God had placed within her at the moment she was conceived. Grandma Moses painted for more than twenty years until her death at the age of 101. I believe, that like Grandma Moses, we all have hidden talents that God wishes us to discover and use for His glory. There is much more to you than you currently know!

Of the four gospels, John wrote the most about (1) what Jesus thought and (2) what Jesus prayed when He was alone. Consider the following examples from the Gospel of John.

**John 2:24-25, "But Jesus, on His part, was not entrusting Himself to them, for He knew all men,
25 and because He did not need anyone to bear witness concerning man for He Himself knew what was in man."**

John 5:6, "When Jesus saw him lying there, and knew that he had already been a long time in that condition, He said to him, "Do you wish to get well?"

John 6:64, "But there are some of you who do not believe. For Jesus knew from the beginning who they were who did not believe, and who it was that would betray Him."

John 13:11, "For He knew the one who was betraying Him; for this reason He said, "Not all of you are clean."

John 16:19, "Jesus knew that they wished to question Him, and He said to them, Are you deliberating together about this, that I said, A little while, and you will not behold Me, and again a little while, and you will see Me? "

How did he know what Jesus thought and prayed? We know that the Holy Spirit told him these things, but why John? Why not Peter or James, the other two closest disciples of Jesus?

John refers to himself four times as "the disciple whom Jesus loved." He had a special, more intimate relationship with Jesus than the other twelve. He is the disciple who was leaning on Jesus' breast at the last supper. Leaning on Jesus' breast, he could hear the heart beat of the Savior! He was the most intimate with Jesus.

He was also the most faithful. John was the only one that went to Jesus' trial and he was the only disciple who stood at the foot of the cross and watched Jesus die. He was the one that Jesus trusted to take care of his mother. When they went fishing, John was the only one who recognized the resurrected Jesus standing on the shore (John 21:7).

Proverbs 3:32 says, "...He is intimate with the upright." John proved to be a faithful, upright man who always stayed near Jesus. When all the others ran, John stayed close. This is why I believe he had the most intimate knowledge of what Jesus thought and prayed.

We need that intimate relationship, that intimate knowledge that comes from always staying near our Lord. We need to know what He knows! The promise of intimacy is there. Walk upright and stay close.

God wants us to draw near. He promises that if we draw near to Him, He will draw near to us. He wants us to draw near because He loves us. He accepts us just as we are, but He loves us so much that He will not leave us the way we are. He wants to make us whole and guide us to fulfillment. Abraham Maslow lists "Self-actualization" or "Self-fulfillment" as the highest level of his "Hierarchy of Human Needs." In order to reach Biblical self-fulfillment, the Lord wishes to set us free from everything that harms us. However, we, the recipients of his grace and love, must be willing and cooperative.

In the early years of our ministry together, my wife and I were asked to join a group of people praying for the healing of a woman who had recently been diagnosed with a very serious type of cancer. Sarah and I were relatively new at all this but we never turned down a request to pray for someone. I had known Gale for a few years. Gale was very respected at work and held a responsible position in her local church. She even participated in monthly gatherings to pray for the sick in the community. I had talked to her many times about God and things she had learned from the Bible.

We met with about four others to pray in Gale's home. After a few moments of prayer, I felt a very strong impression that there was a relationship problem that was hindering Gale's healing. I asked general questions like, "Are you having problems in any of your relationships?" and "Is there anyone who has hurt you and you have trouble forgiving them?" I probed further by asking specifically about parents, brothers and sisters, co-workers, etc. All my answers received a gracious "no." We prayed longer but no one received any specific revelations so we ended our time together.

The next week, Lucy and another friend who had been with us during the prayer time, asked to take me out to lunch. Before we had finished the first course, Lucy asked, "Do you remember last week when you asked Gale, 'Are you having any relationship problems?"

"Yes," I replied matter-of-factly.

"When you said that, I knew she was a dead woman," my friend said firmly.

I felt the muscles in my stomach tightening. "What do you mean?"

I have never forgotten Lucy's explanation. She said, "There are some things people would rather die than face. And, there are some things God will not allow His children to get away with. You never figured out what the relationship problem was, but you were right. The woman Gale lives with is much more than a friend. Gale has been involved with her since university."

In my innocence, I still didn't know what Lucy was talking about. So I asked her to please explain. She simply said, "Gale's friend meets all her needs and Gale would rather die than ever face this."

A sense of hopelessness filled me. I had never felt so sad or helpless. We didn't talk much during the rest of our meal.

Gale's condition deteriorated rapidly. Nothing seemed to slow the onslaught of the cancer. Summoning all my courage, I called Gale's hospital room. She was weakened but still cheerful. I told her I had been praying for her and asked if I could read a few verses to her. I read from **Psalms 51:1-6 which says,**

1 "Be gracious to me, O God, according to Thy lovingkindness; According to the

greatness of Thy compassion blot out my transgressions.

2 Wash me thoroughly from my iniquity, And cleanse me from my sin.

3 For I know my transgressions, And my sin is ever before me.

4 Against Thee, Thee only, I have sinned, And done what is evil in Thy sight, So that Thou art justified when Thou dost speak, And blameless when Thou dost judge.

5 Behold, I was brought forth in iniquity, And in sin my mother conceived me.

6 Behold, Thou dost desire truth in the innermost being, And in the hidden part Thou wilt make me know wisdom."

Gale listened silently as I read. When I finished reading I said, "Gale, you know there is sin that is blocking you from receiving your healing and you know what that sin is, don't you?"

She only said, "Yes."

"Gale, I really believe God wants to heal you but He can't. I've prayed and prayed for your healing but it won't come unless you deal with this."

"Thank you," was her only reply.

I felt terrible inside. I told her I loved her and would keep praying. That was the last time I ever talked to her. I left for a mission trip to India in a few weeks. Gale died while I was gone.

Many people had questions about why God would let such a wonderful Christian die. If God is full of grace and mercy why didn't He heal her? They never knew that Gale HAD received grace and mercy. God's grace revealed the secret and He wanted to set her free. His mercy was extended to her. She made the choice. God loved her so much he would not allow her to continue in a relationship that grieved His heart and was destroying her.

God never reveals hidden things to harm us. If He reveals something, it is His time to set you free and heal you. He's not trying to hurt you all over again or embarrass you. He loves you. His love and His revelations bring healing and wholeness. Never run from the light. Run to the light and be restored.

Principle 3:

If they do it to others, they will do it to you.

"It" means almost anything. From the positive perspective, "it" means if they are generous and loving and kind to others, then they will be that way with you. I hope everyone is blessed with friends and family who do good things. But, it is not the positive actions that make us stumble. It is those unexpected actions from those we thought were our friends.

"It" from the other perspective means that if they have broken relationships with others, they will break with you. If they talked badly about others, they will talk badly about you. If they reject others, they will reject you, too. Don't think you are special!

Jesus said, "if they did it to me, they'll do it to you, too."

John 15:18-20, "If the world hates you, you know that it has hated Me before it hated you.

19 If you were of the world, the world would love its own; but because you are not of the world, but I chose you out of the world, therefore the world hates you.

20 Remember the word that I said to you, 'A slave is not greater than his master.' If they persecuted Me, they will also persecute you; if they kept My word, they will keep yours also."

71

Unless a person is genuinely convicted of his sins, repents and is changed by the Holy Spirit, he is going to do the same thing again and again. He can't help it. Again the Bible uses examples from nature.

2 Peter 2:22, "It has happened to them according to the true proverb, 'A dog returns to its own vomit,' and, 'A sow, after washing, returns to wallowing in the mire.'"

Proverbs 26:11, "Like a dog that returns to its vomit is a fool who repeats his folly."

Jeremiah 13:23, "Can the Ethiopian change his skin or the leopard his spots? Then you also can do good Who are accustomed to doing evil."

A dog returns to its vomit. A clean sow returns to wallowing in the mud. A leopard cannot change his spots. God wants us to understand and provides many examples to help us.

When people come to your church from another church, "Beware!" If they come talking badly about the pastor or other members, then, at some point, they will probably speak the same way about you. And, they will eventually leave you.

Let me quickly add a word of balance here. There are legitimate reasons for leaving one church and going to another. We have several sincere believers in our church in Japan who have left other churches and have become very dear, faithful saints in our own. Most of them left for one of these reasons: (1) The pastor or denomination was too legalistic and controlling; (2) the pastor was not teaching the Bible or teaching things contrary to the Word; or, (3) the church was not open to the work of the Holy Spirit. These are valid reasons that may prompt the Holy Spirit to place you in a new church. I do believe and teach others that it is the work of the Holy Spirit to place us in a church because 1 Corinthians 12:18 says, "But now God has placed the members, each one of them, in the body, just as He desired." Previously Paul stated, "For by one Spirit we were all baptized into one body..." (1 Corinthians 12:13). We are made a member of His body, the church, and placed specifically where He wants us to be at any given point in history. I cannot make myself a member of His body by my own efforts nor do I have the right to just choose to be any part of the body I wish. God calls me, saves me, chooses what gifts to bestow upon me and places me into His body. It is all His doing. Therefore any changes that are made need to be at His clear direction and not just because I am unhappy or uncomfortable. Having made this clear, let's return to our discussion of this principle.

What you must look for is a "pattern of leaving." Some who have come to us and eventually left had already been to two or three other churches before joining us. I have been able to keep track of some of them after they left our church. Some have been to two or three churches since leaving us. When I lived in Alabama we called them "charismatic butterflies." Just like a butterfly, they would light on one flower or church for a short time. Then they would quickly, almost unpredictably, fly to another flower/church. Some of them were always looking for a new or more exciting experience.

Unity in the Body of Christ must be a primary concern of every believer. A disgruntled church member usually brings their dissatisfactions with them. This infected person can spread his discontent like a virus. Let me give you a hypothetical situation regarding a typical method of causing division in a church.

Let's say Gweyne is disappointed in the way Pastor Williams is conducting the mid-week prayer meeting. Gweyne goes to Francis to share her burdens and concerns. Gweyne says to Francis, "Now this is just between you and me." Then she shares what she feels about Pastor Williams and the service. Francis is flattered and feels that she is very special to Gweyne. She keeps the secret, but this has planted a seed of distrust in her heart toward Pastor Williams. Then Gweyne goes to Carol and says, "I have a burden I would like to share with you so you can pray with me. Now this is just between you and me so please don't share it with anyone else." Carol is also flattered that she is trusted enough by Gweyne to share the secret. Now the gossip has spread and a second seed of distrust and suspicion is planted. But Gweyne does not stop there. She goes from person to person spreading the poison of division.

People don't realize that if Gweyne will talk

about Pastor Williams this way, then she will also talk about them in the same way. By this subtle and secretive method great division is sown until many people are hurt and discouraged.

One particular person who had caused much division in my state side church by doing what I just described left our church. She later moved to another city. When I learned that she had joined the church of a friend of mine, I was concerned. While we were on the phone one day, I asked him how she was doing. His comment was, "Oh, you know. Once a crazy, always a crazy." He said she had made several disparaging comments about my wife and I. He informed her he really didn't want to hear those kinds of things. In less than two years she had gotten upset with him and left his church. I'm sure she's still going to church somewhere. Unless she has allowed the Holy Spirit to convict her and make the necessary adjustments in her life, she is still taking people into her confidence and sowing division.

Principle 4:

There are very few faithful, long-term friends.

"Most men will proclaim every one his own goodness: but a faithful man who can find? " Proverbs 20:6 (KJV).

Every year I appreciate my old, faithful friends more and more. There are so many acquaintances with whom I no longer have any contact. It is alright for casual acquaintances to come and go but it is much more difficult when those you have bonded with and thought were faithful, loyal friends are gone.

I have noticed that some people can only stay in a friendship or a church for 2 to 3 years or until a certain level of intimacy is achieved. People set limits and feel threatened when those limits are approached. Then they move on and start over.

As an American living in Japan, I have had to accept that, in society at large, most people will only allow me to get to a certain level. No matter how fluent a foreigner can speak Japanese, there is only so far he can go in normal relationships. Therefore, once a foreigner, you are always a foreigner.

I have to accept that in the greater unsaved community; but, I do not, and I will not, accept that in the community of believers. Ever since coming to Japan we have worked very hard to break down that barrier. Since we founded Living Way Church in 1988, we have striven to make a barrier free environment where intimate relationships can be made without regard to race or nationality. Those who have persevered with us have slowly accepted this vision. Unfortunately, some Japanese and some foreigners have chosen to leave.

As the activity level of the Holy Spirit increases among us, more and more hidden imperfections are exposed. Some people want the power of the Spirit but will abandon ship when the Spirit starts exposing what's in their lives.

There are those who will walk with you for years, and then, one day, walk away with no explanation and have nothing to do with you ever again. There were three Japanese women in our church who were very much involved in the current renewal in Japan until the Holy Spirit started touching what was hidden within them and their families. They walked out, after being with us for years, without any explanation.

If it were only Japanese who did this I could write it off as a cultural enigma. It is not. It's a human being problem, not a cultural problem. Thinking back to the early days of our work in the Charismatic movement I remember a young couple that visited our newly formed church. The husband loved everything about the church but his wife could not handle the openness. When they left us to join a large, mainline, denominational church, they gave one reason. The wife said, "You are too transparent." I genuinely liked that couple and it hurt me when they left. I've always wondered what she did not want anyone to see.

Paul warned Timothy about how people would act in the last days.

2 Timothy 3:1-5, "But realize this, that in the last days difficult times will come.
2 For men will be lovers of self, lovers of money, boastful, arrogant, revilers, disobedient to parents, ungrateful, unholy,
3 unloving, irreconcilable, malicious gossips, without self-control, brutal, haters of good,
4 treacherous, reckless, conceited, lovers of pleasure rather than lovers of God;
5 holding to a form of godliness, although they have denied its power; and avoid such men as these."

"Irreconcilable," *aspondos*, means "without truce; admitting no truce." In other words, they refuse to stop being angry. They refuse to make peace. They insist on staying at war or angry or separated. They refuse to restore the relationship. This is not the heart of God. Jesus had the ministry of reconciliation. And, He passed that ministry on to us.

Please make a special note that the following verses were written to a Christian church, not the local heathens at the pool hall!

2 Corinthians 5:18-20, "Now all these things are from God, who reconciled us to Himself through Christ, and gave us

**the ministry of reconciliation,
19 namely, that God was in Christ
reconciling the world to Himself, not
counting their trespasses against them,
and He has committed to us the word
of reconciliation.
20 Therefore, we are ambassadors for
Christ, as though God were entreating
through us; we beg you on behalf of
Christ, be reconciled to God."**

Paul is actually begging Christians to be reconciled
to God! They don't need to be reconciled in the
way that lost, unsaved people do. Nevertheless,
there is something between them and God that is
hindering their relationship. In his two letters that
we have to the Corinthians, he certainly talks about
enough problems among the believers that could be
separating them from an intimate relationship with
God.

Peter mentions one particular problem between
husbands and wives that can cause a problem in the
man's relationship with God.

**1 Peter 3:7, "You husbands likewise, live
with your wives in an understanding
way, as with a weaker vessel, since she
is a woman; and grant her honor as a
fellow heir of the grace of life, so that
your prayers may not be hindered."
(Amplified Bible) "...in order that
your prayers may not be hindered and**

cut off.--Otherwise you cannot pray effectively."

Saved husbands can need to be reconciled both to God and their wives! If my prayers are cut off, I really have a problem.

Remove all the hindrances between you and God and you and your significant others. David encouraged us to "Trust in the Lord, and do good; Dwell in the land and cultivate faithfulness" [Psalms 37:3]. We all need more long-term, faithful friends so start today to "cultivate faithfulness."

Principle 5:

Logic and common sense do not apply.

Sound reasoning and practical concerns are not accurate predictors of what people will do. Often decisions are based on emotions and the process used to make those decisions are not explained. The guidelines of scripture are not followed nor even considered. Therefore confronting them with what the Word says has little or no effect.

> **2 Timothy 4:1-4, "I solemnly charge you in the presence of God and of Christ Jesus, who is to judge the living and the dead, and by His appearing and His kingdom:**
> **2 preach the word; be ready in season and out of season; reprove, rebuke, exhort, with great patience and instruction.**
> **3 For the time will come when they will not endure sound doctrine; but wanting to have their ears tickled, they will accumulate for themselves teachers in accordance to their own desires;**
> **4 and will turn away their ears from the truth, and will turn aside to myths."**
>
> **(Amplified Bible), v. 3-4, "...but having itching ears [for something pleasing and gratifying], they will**

gather to themselves one teacher after another to a considerable number, chosen to satisfy their own liking and to foster the errors they hold, And will turn aside from hearing the truth and wander off into myths and man-made fictions."

Even though people may not want to hear the Word we still have a responsibility to tell them the truth of the Word. It is not our responsibility to make them obey the Word. It is our responsibility to make sure they know what it says. The rest is between them and God. Let me give you an example.

Charles and I were asked by a young housewife to talk to her husband. The husband had just been fired from his most recent job. They were deeply in debt and had almost no food in the house. Although Charles and I were just a few years older than this couple, we were leaders in the church and had a close relationship with this young man.

Walking from our car we passed the new, expensive Volkswagen Jetta in the drive way. It was a much better car than either of us owned. We were welcomed into the living room by the young wife. Her husband greeted us and turned down the Christian music playing on the new sound system. The room was filled with nice things—almost all of which had been bought on credit.

We talked to this young man about the destructive patterns we saw in his life. This was the eighth or ninth job he had either been fired from or been given the opportunity to resign before he was fired. In each case the reasons were almost the same. He always had a conflict with authority. Usually within a few weeks on a new job he was disagreeing with the boss and/or company procedures and policies. Tension at work always escalated as disagreements frequently turned to out-and-out defiance. His tenure was dependent upon the tolerance and patience of his superior. Some were longsuffering. Others had seen too many know-it-all young men come their way and quickly set them free to be right on their own.

The young husband was not very receptive to our comments. Charles and I tried to persuade him from the Bible about his inability to relate to authority and how that was hurting him and his wife. We talked about his spending habits that were getting him deeper and deeper into debt. The more we quoted the Bible the more irritated he became. Finally he jumped up and shouted, "I don't care what the Bible says, and this is what I want to do!"

Charles and I looked at each other in shock. This was a young man who had gone to a Christian school preparing to be a minister. He had preached to his unsaved father again and again about what the Bible said. Charles looked at me and intoned, "Well... there's nothing else we can say." Thus ended that evening's conversation.

Since the young man was a Christian, we had appealed to him based on what the scriptures said. Not only would he not listen to the scriptures, but he was also defying sound reason. Common sense would tell you that you do not need to keep going in debt when there is not enough food for your wife and baby. You can't eat an elaborate sound system. After losing eight jobs for basically the same reason, common sense would tell you that the problem must be in you, not in your bosses. This young man had moved beyond the Word and all common sense.

I am pleased to report that within a few days the young man called and repented for what he had said. He knew he was wrong and did try to change his behavior. In a moment of anger he blurted out what most Christians would not dare say, "I don't care what the Bible says, this is what I want to do." We wouldn't say that out loud and we may even try to stifle the thought running through our emotions. We just do it and live it. In this way, the young husband was more honest than most of us.

All over the world we are seeing the words of Jesus and Paul lived out before our eyes. People are turning from the absolute truth of God's word. When this happens among Christians, the salt is losing its savor and is no longer preserving or healing those it touches. We must be good salt in the church and in the world.

Mark 9:50, "Salt is good; but if the salt becomes unsalty, with what will you make it salty again? Have salt in yourselves, and be at peace with one another."

The King James Version uses the word "savor." Savor means "to have a particular taste or smell; to exhibit a specified quality or characteristic." Is the reason we have so little peace with one another because we no longer have that special quality or characteristic of Christ about us?

After we moved to Shizuoka city in Japan to start a church, we did not see many of the people we had first worked with in Japan. On one visit to see some old friends we asked a dear older sister, Shizuko, if she had seen one of the young men who had been in a church we helped. In her best broken English she tried to describe what she felt. She summed up the young man by saying, "He doesn't smell like a Christian any more." I'm not exactly sure that is what she meant to say but she communicated the young man's condition very clearly.

When people are with us, do they taste Jesus? Do they smell the heavenly scent of Christ? Are we a sweet aroma of Christ? What does a Christian smell like? Paul gives a brief description for the Corinthians.

2 Corinthians 2:15-16, "For we are a fragrance of Christ to God among those who are being saved and among those who are perishing;
16 to the one an aroma from death to death, to the other an aroma from life to life. And who is adequate for these things?"

The fragrance of Christ is the smell of life. Maybe somewhere in our DNA is buried the memory of that sweet smell of the tree of life. Somehow people recognize that smell of life and respond.

Principle 6:

Almost without warning, shouts of "Hosanna!" can change to shouts of "Crucify!"

Jesus said beware when all men praise you.

Luke 6:26, "Woe to you when all men speak well of you, for in the same way their fathers used to treat the false prophets."

Jesus knew what was in all men and what they were capable of doing.

**John 2:23-25, "Now when He was in Jerusalem at the Passover, during the feast, many believed in His name, beholding His signs which He was doing.
24 But Jesus, on His part, was not entrusting Himself to them, for He knew all men,
25 and because He did not need anyone to bear witness concerning man for He Himself knew what was in man."**

Jesus knew what was coming. He knew that the same people who put down palm branches as He rode into Jerusalem and shouted, "Hosanna!," were the same ones who, only a week later, would be shouting, "Crucify Him!" Therefore He did not entrust Himself to all men, but only a few.

Conrad Philips, a dear pastor friend who has been in the ministry over fifty years, once told me, "Ricky, when a man puts his arms around me and says, 'I love you and I'll always be there for you. You can count on me.' I might as well go strike his name off the church roll right then. He's as good as gone." Unfortunately, his words have been all too true in my own experience.

As the Holy Spirit began to move in our church in Shizuoka in a new way we attracted people who were unhappy with their more traditional, more sedate churches. One Sunday, an older lady who had been with us for about two years came up to hug me after the service. She proceeded to tell me how much she loved me. She said, "Your teaching is so wonderful. I love you. I love your teaching. I love this church more than any I have ever been in." She hugged me as a mother would a son with whom she was very pleased.

Right behind her was a middle-aged woman we had helped through the painful after affects of an unpleasant divorce. She too told me how much she enjoyed the church and my teaching. She talked to me about a young single woman in our church that she was particularly concerned about. When I encouraged her, as an older woman, to reach out to the younger woman and help her, she assured me she would help.

That was the last time I saw either the older lady or the middle-aged one at church. After expressing their great love for both the church and me, neither returned nor had the courtesy to call and say they were leaving. After weeks of not seeing or hearing from them, I had to call them both to ask where they had been. Both informed me, matter-of-factly, that they had joined another church (not the same one, though). I wish I could say I had seen this coming and that I handled it well. The fact was, I did not see it coming at all and I was deeply hurt by their actions. I thought that since they loved the church and me so much they would have at least said goodbye!

Paul warned young Timothy that men would be unfaithful and fall away. Paul knew that from his own experience. But, Paul also told Timothy that even when we are not faithful, God is faithful!

> **2 Timothy 3:1-5, "But realize this, that in the last days difficult times will come.**
> **2 For men will be lovers of self, lovers of money, boastful, arrogant, revilers, disobedient to parents, ungrateful, unholy,**
> **3 unloving, irreconcilable, malicious gossips, without self-control, brutal, haters of good,**
> **4 treacherous, reckless, conceited, lovers of pleasure rather than lovers of God;**
> **5 holding to a form of godliness, although they have denied its power; and avoid such men as these."**

> **2 Timothy 2:13, "If we are faithless, He remains faithful; for He cannot deny Himself."**

Like the writer of Hebrews 12:2 says, "Keep your eyes fixed on Jesus" or as the Amplified Bible says, "Looking away [from all that will distract] to Jesus." Our faith begins and ends in Him. He is the faithful one. Therefore, don't be distracted with what people do. Keep your eyes on Jesus.

A wise and aged missionary teacher used to say, "God has faith in YOU, because God has faith IN you." In other words, God has faith in you because He has placed His faith in you. He trusts in His Faith. He cannot deny Himself or that part of Himself that is in you. Be of good courage. Jesus has promised, "I will never desert you, nor will I ever forsake you" [Hebrews 13:5].

Principle 7:

Uninvolved means unattached.

People who consistently turn down opportunities to serve or take on responsibilities are keeping themselves free to leave. A spectator is not a member. Only participants are true members of the church.

The best evangelist we have in our church is Franklin Green, Frank for short. Before coming to Japan Frank was involved in a ministry that worked predominately with young people on university campuses. His particular group did not consider anyone a member of the church until they were actively involved in some form of serving. This did not mean they had to teach or preach. Their idea was Christ came to serve not to be served. Therefore, if you are a Christian, which means "like Christ," then you will be serving in some way.

One of Frank's first ministries was preparing the coffee and donuts for fellowship times between the first service and second and at the end of the second. This may not sound like much, but Frank had to be sure he had enough coffee and donuts for an average of 300 people a Sunday. This is part of his gift of evangelism. During these fellowship times people came to know the Lord. They opened their lives to others and received guidance and encouragement. Let the coffee and donuts run out and some unsaved, discouraged person may not have the courage to stand around and talk to someone who could show him the path of life. Frank didn't turn this into a "Coffee for Christ" or "Donuts to Deliverance" ministry. He simply served in a practical way and God used his faithfulness.

The very meaning of "fellowship" has to do with partaking together. Fellowship, *koinonia*, is defined as "partnership, i.e., (literal) participation, or (social) intercourse. *(AGES Digital Library Reference, Greek Dictionary of the New Testament by James Strong, S.T.D., LL.D)* Look at some of the many scriptures talking about fellowship.

Acts 2:42, "And they were continually devoting themselves to the apostles' teaching and to fellowship, to the breaking of bread and to prayer."

2 Corinthians 6:14, "Do not be bound together with unbelievers; for what partnership have righteousness and lawlessness, or what fellowship has light with darkness?"

2 Corinthians 13:14, "The grace of the Lord Jesus Christ, and the love of God, and the fellowship of the Holy Spirit, be with you all."

1 John 1:3, "What we have seen and heard we proclaim to you also, that you also may have fellowship with us; and indeed our fellowship is with the Father, and with His Son Jesus Christ."

1 John 1:6-7, "If we say that we have fellowship with Him and yet walk in the darkness, we lie and do not practice the truth;
7 but if we walk in the light as He Himself is in the light, we have fellowship with one another, and the blood of Jesus His Son cleanses us from all sin."

We are called to share in life together, to be partners, to be fellow participants in the life of Christ. I'm reminded of the story about the pastor of a small church who walked hand-in-hand with his little daughter to church. They were the first ones there. As they passed the offering box at the front of the church the daughter watched her father put a dollar bill into the box. After the service the pastor and his daughter were the last ones to leave. He stopped at the offering box to collect the morning tithes. As he pulled out only the one-dollar bill that he himself had put in, a disappointed look crossed his face. His sweet little daughter innocently offered her advice. "Daddy, if you had put more in, you would have gotten more out."

Many do not seem to understand that principle when it comes to life in the body of Christ. We want to get a lot out without putting anything in. I guess that is human nature (old unredeemed, unrenewed mind) to want to get something for nothing. The little girl was right. The more you put in, the more you get out. Except with God's blessings, we can put in 5 loaves and 2 little fishes and get back 12 baskets left over after feeding thousands!

A lady who had been visiting our church for months asked to meet with my wife and I to explain why she wanted to leave the church where she was presently a member and join us. We had two marathon sessions, totaling about seven hours, with this woman as she explained her family and church history. She had even prepared written handouts for us. She was convinced that our church was what she had been looking for all these years. We welcomed her.

Her zeal was unmatched the first four months she was with us. As we identified some of her talents and gifts we offered her opportunities to serve according to her gifting. With each opportunity came an excuse for being unable to serve. We asked her to help in many different ways, but each time she was too busy. She kept herself detached and never accepted even the smallest responsibility. Once when she did agree to do something, on the day she was to do it, someone else showed up. Without talking to me, she had arranged for someone to take her place. Her attendance declined until she disappeared entirely with no comment or explanation. It was easy to leave since she was not involved with any person or any activity.

When my family first moved to Japan we lived with two other families above the church we were helping. It was crowded but a good introduction to life on the mission field in Japan. About once a week the pastor's family would call for a morning of cleaning to tidy up all the things that weren't getting done on a day-to-day basis. Almost every time this call for work came, one lady among us suddenly felt this tremendous burden to intercede. She would leave the rest of us to go downstairs and seek the Lord. We did not want to interfere with her prayer nor hinder someone receiving what they needed because there was no intercessor. After a few weeks it became obvious that these great burdens always coincided with our work time. It was amazing how the burden would lift and victory would come very shortly after all the work was finished. We gradually discerned that it was not the Holy Spirit hindering her involvement in the life of the household.

Before I moved to Japan, one of our faithful attendees called me complaining that she felt left out. She was depressed and wanted advice. She explained that she did not know what her place was in the body of Christ; she did not understand what her gifts and ministry were; and, she did not feel like she really belonged in our fellowship. My wife and I gave her suggestions on ways she could serve in the church. We suggested she help with the children's Sunday school or help with the handicapped lady who attended church but lived in a nursing home. We suggested numerous practical ways of helping. To some of our suggestions she said, "I don't feel led or called to that ministry." To others she replied, "I'll have to pray about that." Like so many others who called with the same complaints, she never "felt led" or "called" to accept any of our suggestions.

Later, I offered her our "Recipe for Overcoming Depression: Isaiah 58." I feel that in a few short verses God has given us some very practical

97

guidelines for gaining victory over the dark shadows
of depression that haunt so many who feel alienated
or disenfranchised. There are also some practical
suggestions for how to get involved.

**Isaiah 58:1-12, "Cry loudly, do not
hold back; Raise your voice like a
trumpet, And declare to My people
their transgression, And to the house of
Jacob their sins.
2 Yet they seek Me day by day, and
delight to know My ways, As a nation
that has done righteousness, And has
not forsaken the ordinance of their
God. They ask Me for just decisions,
They delight in the nearness of God.
3 'Why have we fasted and Thou dost not
see? Why have we humbled ourselves
and Thou dost not notice?' Behold, on
the day of your fast you find your desire,
And drive hard all your workers.
4 Behold, you fast for contention and
strife and to strike with a wicked fist.
You do not fast like you do today to
make your voice heard on high.
5 Is it a fast like this which I choose, a
day for a man to humble himself? Is it
for bowing one's head like a reed, And
for spreading out sackcloth and ashes
as a bed? Will you call this a fast, even
an acceptable day to the Lord?
6 Is this not the fast which I choose, To**

loosen the bonds of wickedness, To undo the bands of the yoke, And to let the oppressed go free, And break every yoke?

7 Is it not to divide your bread with the hungry, And bring the homeless poor into the house; When you see the naked, to cover him; And not to hide yourself from your own flesh?

8 Then your light will break out like the dawn, And your recovery will speedily spring forth; And your righteousness will go before you; The glory of the Lord will be your rear guard.

9 Then you will call, and the Lord will answer; You will cry, and He will say, 'Here I am.' If you remove the yoke from your midst, The pointing of the finger, and speaking wickedness,

10 And if you give yourself to the hungry, And satisfy the desire of the afflicted, Then your light will rise in darkness, And your gloom will become like midday.

11 And the Lord will continually guide you, And satisfy your desire in scorched places, And give strength to your bones; And you will be like a watered garden, And like a spring of water whose waters do not fail.

12 And those from among you will rebuild the ancient ruins; You will raise up the age-old foundations; And you

will be called the repairer of the breach, The restorer of the streets in which to dwell."

This is a wonderful passage of scripture. The phrases "your light will rise in darkness, and your gloom will become like midday" and "your light will break out like the dawn" describe victory over depression and discouragement. The darkness and the gloom and the feeling like God never answers when you cry out sound like what I have heard so often from people in depression. The feeling that God does not see or notice us! Yet, in these verses is a recipe for victory. Follow these steps:

(1) Set others free. This could be literal or it could mean to forgive others who have hurt you. It could even mean stop trying to control others. Set them free.
(2) Feed the hungry.
(3) Bring the homeless poor into the house.
(4) Clothe those without clothing.
(5) Stop pointing the finger at others; stop accusing others and take responsibility for your own actions and short-comings.
(6) Stop speaking badly of others.

If we will do these things then these great benefits will be ours:

(1) Your recovery will speedily spring forth.
(2) Light like the brightness of dawn will drive away the darkness and gloom.

(3) The glory of the Lord will be your rear guard; in other words, He will keep those things in your past that caused all this gloom and doom from overtaking you again.
(4) The Lord will answer you when you cry to Him.
(5) He will continually guide you.
(6) He will satisfy your desire in scorched places.
(7) He will strengthen your bones. The life is in the blood and the blood is produced in the bones!
(8) You will be watered continually, no longer a dried up garden.
(9) You will rebuild and restore what was torn down.

Everyone wants to enjoy all the benefits. The way to the benefits is through being personally involved in the lives of others. As we minister to others, we receive ministry. As we get involved with the needs of others, God gets involved with our needs. The writer of Proverbs declares, "The generous man will be prosperous, And he who waters will himself be watered"(Proverbs 11:25).

In Matthew 10 Jesus is giving instructions to his disciples before sending them out to minister. He tells them,

Matthew 10:7-8, "And as you go, preach, saying, 'The kingdom of heaven is at hand.'
8 Heal the sick, raise the dead, cleanse

the lepers, cast out demons; freely you received, freely give."

He encourages them to give without reservation because that is how they have received from God.

After instructing his disciples, Jesus sends them out to put into practice what they had learned. While they were out ministering to others, Jesus did not just sit at home waiting for them to report back. Matthew 11:1 tells us that, "It came about that when Jesus had finished giving instructions to His twelve disciples, He departed from there to teach and preach in their cities." Jesus went to minister to the disciples' families and friends! The disciples were practicing on strangers while their closest relationships received ministry from the Son of God Himself!

In the early years of our marriage and ministry I was always struggling with keeping a proper balance in my life. Both my wife and I were working, we had small children and we were serving without pay in a church. In addition, I had already started taking mission trips to India during my summer vacations from school. I was hearing and reading a lot about keeping your priorities straight and, particularly, about not neglecting your wife and children. As a young minister I had been admonished by older brothers, and their wives, "Be careful not to neglect your family, and your wife, in particular." Sometimes the demands of work, family and church required physical, mental and spiritual dexterity.

I remember one particular evening after work. Sarah had a problem that needed my attention. I don't remember the details, except that it was one of those situations that required much listening and talking and expressions of empathy. Before we could get beyond the preliminaries of the problem, the telephone rang. It was Cheryl, a dear friend and church member. Candice had called Cheryl crying. The doctors had informed her that they were fairly certain she had a serious form of cancer. She was to go back the next day for further tests to confirm the doctor's diagnosis. Cheryl asked if I would go with her to pray for Candice.

My first thought was, "This is a test. Who am I going to put first, my wife or another woman in need?" My second thought had more to do with panic than concern for either of the ladies! When I explained the situation to Sarah, she felt that Candice's problem was far more serious than her own and she encouraged me to go with Cheryl. That got me off the hook initially but even as I left home, with my wife's blessing, I still had that gnawing feeling that I was not doing the right thing. Had I failed the priority test? Although Sarah had put the other woman's needs above her own, would she, deep down, resent my leaving? I didn't know.

When I saw Candice, I forgot all my personal struggles and focused on encouraging her. She was very afraid. Cheryl and I prayed with her and sought the Lord for a word of encouragement. During the prayer time, I felt like the Holy Spirit told me that the doctors had made a mistake and that Candice did not have cancer. I shared this with her and exhorted her to take hold of the Lord by faith and trust him that

103

she would be fine. Our time ended with her having moved from fear into faith. She had God's peace protecting her heart.

I had peace until I turned into my neighborhood and remembered the troubled wife I had left behind a few hours earlier. The great faith I had had for Candice vanished as I approached my front door. "What am I walking into when I open the door?" I wondered. "Is Sarah going to be angry or will she be depressed and discouraged?" I was almost afraid to go in.

"Hi, how'd it go with Candice?" Sarah's voice was so cheerful it made me suspicious. Was this some wifely ruse? I didn't want to take any chances so I quickly told how upset Candice had been but how the Lord had ministered to her and lifted her out of despair. Sarah seemed genuinely pleased. Finally, I asked, "What happened to you? Although you told me to go you were still struggling when I left? Why are you so happy now?"

"When you left, I knew you were doing the right thing but I was a little disappointed at being left," Sarah explained. "But, right after you drove off, Kent Barber called. I haven't heard from him in ages. He said he felt like God wanted him to check on me so he called to ask how I was doing. I told him about my problem and he knew exactly what to do. So, I'm fine."

I was so relieved and encouraged. It was also a very valuable lesson. I have learned that even with all the teaching and learning on setting priorities there are still many situations that just do not allow us to make quick, easy decisions. The only sure way to set your priorities right is to hear the Shepherd's voice and obey. When we do what He is calling us to do, then he will take care of those closest to us. Of course, there is no excuse for neglecting your family but if everyone is seeking to follow the Lord then He will see that everyone gets their needs met.

The more involved we are with what Jesus is doing, the more involved He is with us! When we feel Jesus is involved with us, we feel loved and accepted. When we feel loved and accepted it is much easier for us to give to others. It's a wonderful cycle.

Jesus, being the Head of the Body, is deeply concerned about and involved with His Body, the church. Therefore, the more we are involved in the church, the more we are in contact with Him and the more we experience having our own needs met.

Let me add that Candice went back to the doctor the next day and had her tests. They did not confirm what the doctor had suspected. She did not have cancer but rather a condition that was not life threatening and could be treated.

Principle 8:

Actions are more reliable than words.

"Even a child is known by his doings, whether his work be pure, and whether it be right." Proverbs 20:11(KJV).

A person's consistent actions are ten times more reliable than their words. Words with deeds are trustworthy; deeds without words are helpful; but, words without deeds are useless. James explains this quite well.

James 2:14,17-18, 20,22, 24, 26
14 "What use is it, my brethren, if a man says he has faith, but he has no works? Can that faith save him?
17 Even so faith, if it has no works, is dead, being by itself.
18 But someone may well say, 'You have faith, and I have works; show me your faith without the works, and I will show you my faith by my works.'
20 But are you willing to recognize, you foolish fellow, that faith without works is useless?
22 You see that faith was working with his works, and as a result of the works, faith was perfected;
24 You see that a man is justified by works, and not by faith alone.

26 For just as the body without the spirit is dead, so also faith without works is dead."

I remember a cartoon once showing a man wearing a very bright, plaid sports coat. The person talking to him said, "Your coat is so loud I can't hear what you are saying!" All too often our actions, and that may include what we wear or DON'T wear, drown out any words we say. How many fathers, with a cigarette in their hand, tell their son, "Don't ever start smoking son. These things will kill you." Years later the father is disappointed to find an empty cigarette pack in his son's coat pocket. "Do as I say, not as I do" is rarely effective. Children imitate what they see much more than what they hear.

Jesus was a perfect example. He said, "I only do what I see my father do and I only speak what I hear him speak."

John 5:19, "Jesus therefore answered and was saying to them, "Truly, truly, I say to you, the Son can do nothing of Himself, unless it is something He sees the Father doing; for whatever the Father does, these things the Son also does in like manner."

John 8:28, "Jesus therefore said, When you lift up the Son of Man, then you will know that I am He, and I do nothing on My own initiative, but I speak these

things as the Father taught Me."

John 12:49, "For I did not speak on My own initiative, but the Father Himself who sent Me has given Me commandment, what to say, and what to speak."

He could honestly say to Philip, "If you have seen me, you have seen the Father"(John 14:9). "Like father, like son" was perfectly true with him.

John the Baptist said in Luke 3:8:

"Bring forth therefore fruits worthy of repentance, and begin not to say within yourselves, We have Abraham to our father: for I say unto you, That God is able of these stones to raise up children unto Abraham."

John is saying, "Let me see something. Talk is cheap. If you have really repented, put your words into action."

Jesus told the story about the Good Samaritan to illustrate the importance of putting actions to words.

Luke 10:30-37, "Jesus replied and said, A certain man was going down from Jerusalem to Jericho; and he fell among robbers, and they stripped him and beat him, and went off leaving him half dead. 31 And by chance a certain priest was going down on that road, and when he

saw him, he passed by on the other side.

32 And likewise a Levite also, when he came to the place and saw him, passed by on the other side.

33 But a certain Samaritan, who was on a journey, came upon him; and when he saw him, he felt compassion,

34 and came to him, and bandaged up his wounds, pouring oil and wine on them; and he put him on his own beast, and brought him to an inn, and took care of him.

35 And on the next day he took out two denarii and gave them to the innkeeper and said, 'Take care of him; and whatever more you spend, when I return, I will repay you.'

36 Which of these three do you think proved to be a neighbor to the man who fell into the robbers' hands?

37 And he said, 'The one who showed mercy toward him.' And Jesus said to him, Go and do the same."

If you had talked to the Priest or the Levite they would have said the right things and, perhaps, had already taught others what to do; but Jesus asked which one "proved to be a neighbor to the man?" The one who "showed mercy" was the true neighbor, not the ones who simply talked about mercy. He ends with a command, "Go and do the same."

We must give actions precedence over words.

Speaking the correct words is very important, but the actions that follow the words are a truer indication of what is real. Paul told the Corinthians that when he came among them again he wanted to see the reality of the power of God in their lives, not just hear their words.

1 Corinthians 4:19-20, "But I will come to you soon, if the Lord wills, and I shall find out, not the words of those who are arrogant, but their power.
20 For the kingdom of God does not consist in words, but in power."

A brother who traveled frequently in Asia once told about a church in Taiwan. It seems that a very wealthy, prominent businessman in the city had become a Christian. After a short time in the church the businessman asked to meet with the elders of the assembly. He told them that he wanted to join the church and that he would like to give a large contribution as an offering. The elders talked among themselves briefly and then told the businessman, "We feel it best that you keep your gift right now. If you really want to be a part of our fellowship, we welcome you. The men meet every Saturday morning to clean the church. Please join us for work and fellowship."

If you know anything about Chinese culture, you know that the wealthy do not do low manual labor. To everyone's surprise the businessman joined his fellow men every Saturday morning to scrub the floors, clean the toilets and set up the chairs. Some months later the elders called the businessman in and said to him, "You may now give your offering if you wish." They were convinced, by his actions and not by his words, that he really was born again and that he was truly placed among them by the Lord.

How many elders or pastors would have asked a man to wait to give a large sum of money to the church? We would have said, "That's action enough. Where's the money?" Of course money is necessary to the functioning of the church but it is much easier for some people to share their money than their life. Many would rather pay than serve. Many would rather pay than go. A friend of mine used to joke, "I'll be glad to support you as a missionary as long as I don't have to go!" I always appreciated his financial blessing but that can never take the place of God's call on his life or anyone else's.

Principle 9:

Children are a litmus test of character.

The way children respond to adults and the adult's attitudes toward children are indicators of character. People who don't like children and/or are disliked by children have some unresolved issues they need to address. Children are feelers, sensors. They aren't snowed by outward appearances for very long. Jesus never married and fathered children yet he loved children and they loved him. They felt His love and acceptance and wanted to draw near to Him.

God's overall plan was for a man to marry a woman and have children. Eunuchs are rare--they are the exception, not the norm. Jesus was a eunuch and he loved children.

Matthew 19:12-15, "For there are eunuchs who were born that way from their mother's womb; and there are eunuchs who were made eunuchs by men; and there are also eunuchs who made themselves eunuchs for the sake of the kingdom of heaven. He who is able to accept this, let him accept it.
13 Then some children were brought to Him so that He might lay His hands on them and pray; and the disciples rebuked them.
14 But Jesus said, Let the children alone, and do not hinder them from coming to

**Me; for the kingdom of heaven belongs
to such as these.
15 And after laying His hands on them,
He departed from there."**

There is no Bible principle of not having children
for the sake of the ministry. If you don't get married
and don't have children for the kingdom's sake, that
is fine. But if you get married, the normal pattern
is to have children unless you are prevented from
doing so by natural causes. Married without children
was a curse in the Old Testament. I do not want to
condemn in any way those who have tried to have
children and cannot. My concern is with those who
are able to reproduce but choose not to. I believe
they need to carefully consider the underlying issues
of their choice.

When our family first moved to Japan we met
Chester and Sakura. Chester was a zealous faith
preacher with a burning desire to heal the sick and
save the lost. Over the next few years we saw them
at various conferences and had them stay in our
home several times. When we asked them about
starting a family, they said they had decided not to
have children for the sake of the ministry. Neither of
them were particularly young anymore and Sakura
was rapidly reaching the time where she would have
no choice but to remain childless. She really seemed
to enjoy our children so it didn't seem quite right
that they not have any of their own. Chester was
rather adamant though that having children would be
detrimental to them fulfilling the call on their lives.

Over the next few years we would hear from Chester. He usually talked about how lonely he was and how much he needed to be in closer relationship with others. Emotionally he see-sawed between lonely, discouraged lows and exuberant, faith-filled highs. Even though I would encourage him on the telephone, those conversations never developed into anything more between us. I learned later that a missionary from the same country as Chester had offered his church to be a base of operations for him and Sakura so they would have a covering and support. For one reason or another, Chester never would move to the city and work out of that church.

Years later, when I had not heard from Chester in some time, I called the pastor who had offered them support. The pastor, with distress in his voice, told me that Chester and Sakura had gone back to Chester's home country in discouragement. Last we heard Chester was drinking heavily and he and Sakura had separated. We learned later that he had been married and divorced before marrying Sakura, a secret he had not revealed to any of us he worked with in Japan.

Chester's spiritual sounding declaration that, "we will not have children for the sake of the ministry," was just a smoke screen to cover his real problems. Because of the pain and fear of his past, he was unable to commit himself to any long term, close relationships. Not having children had nothing to do with his calling or ministry. He needed healing and freedom for himself. Instead of getting the help he could have received by committing himself to the pastor and church, he chose to remain separate and independent.

In the Amplified Bible, Proverbs 18:1 says, "He who willfully separates and estranges himself [from God and man] seeks his own desire and pretext to break out against all wise and sound judgment." Chester willfully separated himself and his wife from close fellowship as he sought to fulfill his own desires. Eventually, he was not only estranged from his fellow believers but also from God. I believe it was Chester, not Chester and Sakura, who decided not to have children.

I do not say absolutely that every married couple must have children. Neither do I say that every believer must become a missionary. However, I do say absolutely that every believer must be open to having children and open to becoming a missionary. Being open to whatever God wills for your life is not nearly as strong as what Paul said. Paul reminds us that when we are born again we have "been freed from sin,[and] you became slaves of righteousness." [Romans 6:18] To the Corinthians he wrote, "For you have been bought with a price: therefore glorify God in your body"(1 Corinthians 6:20). We are slaves bought and paid for by the death of Jesus Christ on the cross. Therefore, my money, my time, my very life are at His disposal. I am not only to be open, but totally obedient to His every desire. If He says to give money, I give money; but, if He says give your money and go do also, then I better do both. Be open to hear and quick to obey.

Jesus loved the children. He rebuked the disciples for turning them away and commanded them to bring the children near.

Mark 10:14-16, "But when Jesus saw this, He was indignant and said to them, Permit the children to come to Me; do not hinder them; for the kingdom of God belongs to such as these.
15 Truly I say to you, whoever does not receive the kingdom of God like a child shall not enter it at all.
16 And He took them in His arms and began blessing them, laying His hands upon them. "

Look at how Jesus related to the children. He drew them close to Himself. He touched them. The image was that He held them on his lap. He blessed them. Jesus brought them into His intimate zone and demonstrated loving, caring behavior. He sat down and made eye contact. He got on their level to communicate in a non-threatening way. No wonder they loved Him.

I only have a few pictures of my grandfather Gordon, who I called "D". My favorite picture of "D" is of him sitting on a high stool at his small gas and bait station holding my baby daughter right in front of him. He was smiling and making direct eye contact. She was grinning from ear to ear, clearly enjoying the attention from someone she loved and trusted. "D" had a remarkable way with children.

When a child met him for the first time they were

sometimes frightened by his loud voice (for he spoke loud enough that he could hear) and his large size (he was, to be politically correct, horizontally challenged). Even if the child did not want to become friends or even get close, "D" proceeded undeterred. He would usually pick them up, hold them and look right into their eyes as he talked to them with a softer, slightly higher pitched voice. Within a few minutes they were friends. Almost always (if they were old enough) he would offer them a grape drink from his coke machine. He won over each of my children that way. The same way Jesus did. He brought them right into his intimate zone. He got down on their level or brought them up to his. He got personal in a loving, caring way. And, like Jesus, he blessed them.

"According to the US Census Office, the world population on 31 December 2000 was just under 6.12 billion. 63% of the world population—3.8 billion people—are under 34 years old. Yesterday's youth culture is becoming mainstream, with similar values, a common language (English) and a common communication medium (the Internet) around the globe." *(Island Christian Info, Volume 8 No. 2, February, 2001, Victoria, BC, p. 16 www.islandchristianinfo.ca)* An increasing number of those under 34 are children.

Research studies by Youth With A Mission (Y.W.A.M.) indicate that high school students in North America are already hardened against the gospel in many cases. Frank Naea, the first international president of YWAM from Asia, shared at the YWAM National Staff Conference in Japan in March of 2001. He shared that the most recent statistics released by the Billy Graham Evangelistic Association reported that 85% of those making first time decisions in their meetings were between the ages of 4 and 14. He challenged those present to place 85% of their evangelistic efforts at reaching those ages.

In 1999 I talked to one of the local Navigator leaders in Shizuoka who has worked with university students for years. He confirmed that Japanese university students were becoming increasingly difficult to reach except for one particular group. His workers found that if a university student had at least one positive experience with Christianity prior to coming to university, they were still open to the gospel. This is true in my own experience in Japan. If a person has good memories of going to Sunday school or having a friend or English teacher who was a Christian, they are much more open to hearing about Jesus in later years.

It is therefore very important that we reach children with the good news of God's love and salvation. We need to sow good seeds into the lives of as many children as possible. My family has just recently seen the power of such sowing.

I received an e-mail from Mariko, a twenty year old Japanese girl going to school in America. She said, "I just wanted you to know that I am going to church now and studying the Bible. For many years I thought I had to earn God's love and do things. Now I realize that he was there all the time, loving me and calling me to him. I just wanted to let you know." Even now it makes me cry to read this. I remember her journey so well.

One Sunday morning in 1988, when our church was only a few weeks old, 8 year old Mariko was the only person who came. So our family met with Mariko in our little room set aside for the church. The whole message was aimed at explaining the gospel to her. At the end she prayed the sinners prayer. She became good friends with my oldest daughter who was about the same age.

When Mariko's father learned she was interested in Christianity he got very angry. He called for me to come to his house where he explained that he and his family were Buddhists and he did not want his children becoming Christians. He forbade her to come to church and severely limited her interaction with our family. Mariko used to hide her Bible behind her schoolbooks to read. After a few years, her interest waned as she got more involved with school and activities. We almost lost contact with her when we moved to another part of town. But the seeds were there.

Last year God orchestrated a series of events and encounters that caused those seeds to spring to life and grow. He had never let go of her. Like she said, "He was there all the time, loving her and calling her to Himself." She came to see us last year when she was home for a few days. I have never felt so blessed as to be a part of what God has done in her life. She even had the courage to tell her father that she is now a Christian. This time he told her to just do what she wanted to do. She is involved in a good church and studying the Bible faithfully now.

Don't ever look at children as little beings to be tolerated until they can grow up. Too many churches, particularly here in Japan, think of children's ministry as babysitting. We must not lose this golden opportunity to reach them before the world hardens their hearts to the truth.

Also, pay attention to how children and adults interact. You can learn a lot about the character of an adult by how they relate to children. Be alert and learn.

Principle 10:

People faithful in small things will be faithful in larger things.

People who will not follow simple, relatively unimportant instructions will later violate more complex or more important instructions. Jesus said in Luke 16:10-12,

> **"He who is faithful in a very little thing is faithful also in much; and he who is unrighteous in a very little thing is unrighteous also in much.**
> **11 If therefore you have not been faithful in the use of unrighteous mammon, who will entrust the true riches to you?**
> **12 And if you have not been faithful in the use of that which is another's, who will give you that which is your own?"**

In a parable about a nobleman recorded in Luke 19:11-26, Jesus gives another example of being faithful. Jesus tells of a nobleman who called 10 of his slaves and gave them each a mina and told them, "Do business with this until I come back" (v. 13). When he returns he orders the 10 slaves to appear before him and give an account. This is what was said in Luke 19:16-26.

"And the first appeared, saying, 'Master, your mina has made ten minas more.'

17 And he said to him, 'Well done, good slave, because you have been faithful in a very little thing, be in authority over ten cities.'

18 And the second came, saying, 'Your mina, master, has made five minas.'

19 And he said to him also, 'And you are to be over five cities.'

20 And another came, saying, 'Master, behold your mina, which I kept put away in a handkerchief;

21 for I was afraid of you, because you are an exacting man; you take up what you did not lay down, and reap what you did not sow.'

22 He said to him, 'By your own words I will judge you, you worthless slave. Did you know that I am an exacting man, taking up what I did not lay down, and reaping what I did not sow?

23 'Then why did you not put the money in the bank, and having come, I would have collected it with interest?'

24 And he said to the bystanders, 'Take the mina away from him, and give it to the one who has the ten minas.'

25 And they said to him, 'Master, he has ten minas already.'

26 I tell you, that to everyone who has shall more be given, but from the one

**who does not have, even what he does
have shall be taken away."**

In this parable the nobleman/master who goes
away and returns is Jesus. The slaves represent those
who serve Jesus. Each was given the same amount.
Jesus did not rebuke the one who only earned five
minas for not earning ten minas like the first. To both
he said, "'Well done, good slave." Each received a
reward. Each of the ten slaves had equal money and
equal opportunity. They did not have equal ability.
They were rewarded according to how well each
used his own ability making the most of what he had.
The only slave rebuked is the one who did nothing!

We recognize that in the kingdom of God we are
not all created with equal ability. Some are more
naturally talented and gifted. Some are handsome or
beautiful and others are not. Some are very intelligent
and learn easily while others struggle for all they
accomplish. Yet each of us has the same access to
the Father. Each of us has the help of the Holy Spirit.
God does not expect us to be the same or do all the
same things. He does expect us to do the best we can
with what He provides. He expects us to be faithful
in what we receive, not just do nothing. He wants us
to be faithful and obedient. He is the Master; we are
the slave.

King Saul is a good example of a man who would
not be completely obedient, and therefore, not completely
faithful. Saul would not do 100% of what he was told but
would always change something. He did not see complete
obedience and faithfulness as important.

125

1 Samuel 13 describes a difficult situation for Saul. The Philistines have come against him. His men are afraid and start to scatter. Saul has been instructed to wait for Samuel to come offer a sacrifice to the Lord before he goes into battle. Yet, Samuel is slow in coming. Saul decides to take things into his own hands.

1 Samuel 13:8-14, "Now he waited seven days, according to the appointed time set by Samuel, but Samuel did not come to Gilgal; and the people were scattering from him.

9 So Saul said, 'Bring to me the burnt offering and the peace offerings.' And he offered the burnt offering.

10 And it came about as soon as he finished offering the burnt offering, that behold, Samuel came; and Saul went out to meet him and to greet him.

11 But Samuel said, 'What have you done?' And Saul said, Because I saw that the people were scattering from me, and that you did not come within the appointed days, and that the Philistines were assembling at Michmash,

12 therefore I said, 'Now the Philistines will come down against me at Gilgal, and I have not asked the favor of the Lord.' So I forced myself and offered the burnt offering.

13 And Samuel said to Saul, You have

acted foolishly; you have not kept the commandment of the Lord your God, which He commanded you, for now the Lord would have established your kingdom over Israel forever.
14 But now your kingdom shall not endure. The Lord has sought out for Himself a man after His own heart, and the Lord has appointed him as ruler over His people, because you have not kept what the Lord commanded you."

Saul explains his actions that seem fully justified in his eyes. Samuel sees it very differently. Samuel says, "You have acted foolishly; you have not kept the commandment of the Lord your God, which He commanded you..." This is a pattern in Saul's life. He never fully obeys the commandment of the Lord. He always obeys some, but never completely. He always has a way of justifying his actions. They make perfectly good sense to him and probably did to some of his men.

God looked at Saul's actions and into Saul's heart. He indicated that Saul did not have a heart that was like His own. Saul always reserved the right to judge God's commands. If he deemed the command not quite appropriate for the situation, he adjusted the command to suit his own purpose. God saw this as rebellion. Saul was not a man He could trust. He was not faithful to obey in the little things. Therefore, God said He would seek out another to rule.

The story told in I Samuel 15 further illustrates

Saul's tendency to obey most of what the Lord commanded but not all. God spoke through Samuel and instructed Saul to attack Amalek and "utterly destroy all that he has, and do not spare him; but put to death both man and woman, child and infant, ox and sheep, camel and donkey" (I Samuel 15:3). Saul and his army defeat the Amalekites and execute all the people. However, they did not fully obey the command of the Lord.

1 Samuel 15:9-31, "But Saul and the people spared Agag and the best of the sheep, the oxen, the fatlings, the lambs, and all that was good, and were not willing to destroy them utterly; but everything despised and worthless, that they utterly destroyed.
10 Then the word of the Lord came to Samuel, saying,
11 I regret that I have made Saul king, for he has turned back from following Me, and has not carried out My commands. And Samuel was distressed and cried out to the Lord all night.
12 And Samuel rose early in the morning to meet Saul; and it was told Samuel, saying, 'Saul came to Carmel, and behold, he set up a monument for himself, then turned and proceeded on down to Gilgal.'
13 And Samuel came to Saul, and Saul said to him, 'Blessed are you of the

Lord! I have carried out the command
of the Lord.'

14 But Samuel said, 'What then is this
bleating of the sheep in my ears, and
the lowing of the oxen which I hear?'

15 And Saul said, 'They have brought
them from the Amalekites, for the
people spared the best of the sheep and
oxen, to sacrifice to the Lord your God;
but the rest we have utterly destroyed.'

16 Then Samuel said to Saul, 'Wait, and
let me tell you what the Lord said to me
last night.' And he said to him, 'Speak!'

17 And Samuel said, 'Is it not true,
though you were little in your own eyes,
you were made the head of the tribes
of Israel? And the Lord anointed you
king over Israel,

18 and the Lord sent you on a mission,
and said, Go and utterly destroy the
sinners, the Amalekites, and fight against
them until they are exterminated.

19 Why then did you not obey the voice of
the Lord, but rushed upon the spoil and
did what was evil in the sight of the Lord?'

20 Then Saul said to Samuel, 'I did
obey the voice of the Lord, and went on
the mission on which the Lord sent me,
and have brought back Agag the king
of Amalek, and have utterly destroyed
the Amalekites.

21 But the people took some of the spoil,

sheep and oxen, the choicest of the things devoted to destruction, <u>to sacrifice to the Lord your God</u> at Gilgal.'

22 And Samuel said, 'Has the Lord as much delight in burnt offerings and sacrifices As in obeying the voice of the Lord? <u>Behold, to obey is better than sacrifice, And to heed than the fat of rams.</u>

23 <u>For rebellion is as the sin of divination, And insubordination is as iniquity and idolatry.</u> Because you have rejected the word of the Lord, He has also rejected you from being king.'

24 Then Saul said to Samuel, 'I have sinned; I have indeed transgressed the command of the Lord and your words, <u>because I feared the people and listened to their voice.</u>

25 Now therefore, please pardon my sin and return with me, that I may worship the Lord.'

26 But Samuel said to Saul, 'I will not return with you; for you have rejected the word of the Lord, and the Lord has rejected you from being king over Israel.'

27 And as Samuel turned to go, Saul seized the edge of his robe, and it tore.

28 So Samuel said to him, 'The Lord has torn the kingdom of Israel from you today, and has given it to your neighbor who is better than you.

29 And also the Glory of Israel will not lie or change His mind; for He is not a man that He should change His mind.'
30 Then he said, 'I have sinned; but please honor me now before the elders of my people and before Israel, and go back with me, that I may worship <u>the Lord your God</u>.'
31 So Samuel went back following Saul, and Saul worshiped the Lord."
[Underline added by author.]

Saul says he has obeyed the Lord's commandment (v20). Samuel makes it clear that only 100% obedience is considered obedience and nothing less. Samuel expresses the heart of the Lord when he says, "Behold, to obey is better than sacrifice, And to heed than the fat of rams. For rebellion is as the sin of divination, And insubordination is as iniquity and idolatry"(v.22-23). But once again Saul justifies his actions. He says he was afraid of the people and listened to what they said. If this was true, he feared the people more than he feared God. He lost the kingdom because he would not fully obey the Lord. He would not be faithful in the details, in the small things, and therefore God would not give him a kingdom that endured beyond his reign.

A key to Saul's persistent disobedience can be found in the little phrase repeated in verses 21 and 30. When talking to others, Saul continually referred to God as "the Lord **your** God." Never once in scripture does Saul refer to God as "the Lord **my**

God." Saul never seems to have made that transition from serving Samuel's God to serving "his God." He never developed that personal relationship that would have saved both him and his kingdom.

In contrast, listen to the words of David. Notice how personal and intimate his relationship with God was compared to his predecessor.

> **2 Samuel 22:1-3, "And David spoke the words of this song to the Lord in the day that the Lord delivered him from the hand of all his enemies and from the hand of Saul.**
> **2 And he said, The Lord is <u>my rock</u> and <u>my fortress</u> and <u>my deliverer;</u>**
> **3 <u>My God, my rock,</u> in whom I take refuge<u>; My shield and the horn of my salvation, my stronghold and my refuge; My savior,</u> Thou dost save me from violence."**
> *[Underline added by author.]*

> **2 Samuel 22:7, "In my distress I called upon the Lord, Yes, I cried to <u>my God;</u> And from His temple He heard my voice, And my cry for help came into His ears."**
> *[Underline added by author.]*

> **2 Samuel 22:47, "The Lord lives, and blessed be <u>my rock;</u> And exalted be God, the <u>rock of my salvation.</u>"**
> *[Underline added by author.]*

In the Psalms David makes references to God using the personal pronoun "my" over 110 times! God called David, "a man after His own heart." David had a very personal, living relationship with God. His obedience came from that personal relationship that Saul never had. As a result of his obedience in the small things, God established David's kingdom forever. Jesus was a direct descendent of David and thus David's kingdom is eternal.

My wife, Sarah, has been the director of Ai no Kesshin, Loving Decisions in English, for more than 7 years now. We are always in need of volunteer workers to help us work with women in crisis, usually pregnant women. Our number one problem, other than not having enough workers, is finding people who will faithfully follow the instructions they receive. Because we are often dealing with the laws of two different countries when placing an infant for adoption, it is critical that a volunteer do exactly what they are told to do in filling out forms and writing documents. Sarah has worked for years, learning often by trial-and-error, to understand what the Japanese government wants and how they want it done. She explains the procedures to the worker, gives them very precise written instructions and allows them to ask questions again and again before they go out to handle a case.

In spite of her thorough instructions, she has received paperwork incorrectly filled out and learned that her careful instructions were changed or ignored during interviews. In most of the cases, regardless of the nationality or language of the worker, the most common explanation she receives for violating her instructions is "I thought this was a better way to do it in this situation." Even though she tells people very clearly, "Do not change anything. Do it only this way," people still feel free to do things their way. In most cases, she has to go back and spend hours and hours relocating people and redoing forms that are now unacceptable to one or more governmental agencies. Family courts, passport officers and city hall officials do not accept incorrectly filled out papers just because someone thought they had a better way to fill in a document. Yet, again and again, kind hearted, well-intentioned volunteers think it is not that important to follow instructions completely.

King Saul never thought it was that important either. Again and again he would do most of what God instructed him to do. He always had a good reason for not faithfully doing everything exactly God's way. In the end it cost him his life, the lives of his sons and the loss of his kingdom.

In the church we are looking for people who are faithful in the little things first. For many this is a principle they must learn. For those with Saul's fatal flaw, early detection prevents later disasters. Problems need to be detected and corrected now. Those who always justify their actions and do not change their behavior should not be placed in positions of authority. They cannot be trusted.

Principle 11:

True servants are rare.

In almost every country, in almost every church, 10% of the people will do 90% of the work. Another 1%, who won't do anything, will find fault no matter what the 10% do. This is my own observation and not based on a scientific survey. I do remember, just a few weeks before leaving for the mission field, hearing Bjorn Gabriel of Denmark share that in all his travels, as well as in his home church in Copenhagen, he had found that the same 10% of the members would show up for everything. The other 90% felt free to say no, particularly to work or pray, any time they pleased. I have watched for this and have also found it to be a general rule wherever I have traveled.

We see this pretty much the same in the life of Christ. Out of his 12 disciples, 1 complained about the use of the money and became His betrayer. Thousands followed Jesus before His crucifixion. Over 500 saw him at one time after his resurrection [I Corinthians 15:6]. Yet, only 120 were still waiting in the upper room when the Holy Spirit was poured out at Pentecost.

Out of all the people Paul worked with, he had very few that he could genuinely trust to serve diligently and faithfully. He says this about Timothy.

Philippians 2:19-22, "But I hope in the Lord Jesus to send Timothy to you shortly, so that I also may be encouraged

**when I learn of your condition.
20 For I have no one else of kindred
spirit who will genuinely be concerned
for your welfare.
21 For they all seek after their own
interests, not those of Christ Jesus.
22 But you know of his proven
worth that he served with me in the
furtherance of the gospel like a child
serving his father."**

Paul says he has no one else like Timothy. He had
the same spirit as Paul. He would be genuinely
concerned about their well-being. Other people
were more interested in their own well-being, but not
Timothy. Timothy had proven his worth by serving
Paul just like a child serving his father. Paul and
Timothy had a special, father-son relationship.

In writing to the Ephesian church about
parent-child relationships, Paul wrote:

**Ephesians 6:1-2, "Children, obey your
parents in the Lord, for this is right.
2 Honor your father and mother (which is
the first commandment with a promise)."**

There is a difference between "obeying" and
"honoring." Obeying is very important but "honoring"
goes beyond doing what you are told. To honor is
to respect and value. Honoring your parents means
valuing their input into your life and respecting their
counsel and wishes. To honor means to heed not only

direct commands but to consider the wishes and intent of advice given and follow that as well.

Some years ago many Christians in America wore small bracelets stamped or embroidered with "WWJD." "WWJD" means "What Would Jesus Do?" The purpose of the bracelets was to remind the wearer to not only obey the "commandments" in the Bible but also to consider "what would Jesus do" in this situation. Based on a living relationship with Jesus, and with the help of the Holy Spirit, we should be able to envision what He would do in our situation. We should honor his wishes in our circumstances.

My oldest son, Chris, is 26 years old and my youngest, Matison, is 7. I have a different way of relating to each. With Matison, I am in the process of training him to obey. He receives mostly commands. Chris, on the other hand, is a legal adult with a strong desire to be his own man. I rarely command Chris to do anything. Instead, I offer advice and suggestions. However, since Chris and I have a good relationship and he really believes in obeying the word, he does try to honor my counsel. He may not always agree with my advice but he rarely goes against it. We are both still adjusting to a mature, father-son relationship.

Paul did not have the same relationship with others that he enjoyed with Timothy. With Apollos he made suggestions.

1 Corinthians 16:10-12, "Now if Timothy comes, see that he is with you without cause to be afraid; for he is doing the Lord's work, as I also am.

**11 Let no one therefore despise him. But send him on his way in peace, so that he may come to me; for I expect him with the brethren.
12 But concerning Apollos our brother, I encouraged him greatly to come to you with the brethren; and it was not at all his desire to come now, but he will come when he has opportunity."**

Paul had not discipled Apollos. Priscilla and Aquila had had more input into Apollos' life. Paul and Apollos worked together more as equals. But when Paul needed to send someone he knew would not only obey him but also have the same heart as himself, he sent Timothy.

Jesus is our perfect example of a true servant. Jesus, left his place in heaven, became a man like us and took on the role of a bond-servant.

**Philippians 2:5-8, "Have this attitude in yourselves which was also in Christ Jesus,
6 who, although He existed in the form of God, did not regard equality with God a thing to be grasped,
7 but emptied Himself, taking the form of a bond-servant, and being made in the likeness of men.
8 And being found in appearance as a man, He humbled Himself by becoming obedient to the point of death, even death on a cross."**

A bond-servant was one who willingly made himself the servant of another. He had a choice and he chose to become the life-long servant of his master.

Jesus explained to his disciples that when you have only done what you are commanded to do you are still unprofitable as His servant.

Luke 17:10 (KJV), "So likewise ye, when ye shall have done all those things which are commanded you, say, We are unprofitable servants: we have done that which was our duty to do."

"Unprofitable" means "useless." A profitable servant goes beyond his orders. He seeks to follow his master's wishes and honor his will in every situation.

When the disciples were talking about who would be the greatest in the kingdom, Jesus said, "…the Son of Man did not come to be served, but to serve, and to give His life a ransom for many" (Matthew 20:28).

At the last supper, Jesus washed the disciples feet, a job usually performed by the lowest servant in a man's house. Then Jesus explained what He had done.

John 13:12-17, "And so when He had washed their feet, and taken His garments, and reclined at the table again, He said to them, Do you know what I have done to you?
13 You call Me Teacher and Lord; and you are right, for so I am.

139

14 If I then, the Lord and the Teacher, washed your feet, you also ought to wash one another's feet.
15 For I gave you an example that you also should do as I did to you.
16 Truly, truly, I say to you, a slave is not greater than his master; neither is one who is sent greater than the one who sent him.
17 If you know these things, you are blessed if you do them."

Jesus says clearly that He is the example and we are to do just as He did. He is the master and we are the slave. If the master serves, then surely the slaves must serve. He promises we will be blessed if we "do" these things, not just preach and teach about them.

Pastor Mel Glover of Living Word Fellowship was talking about being a servant to his congregation. He said he and his wife had been to a very expensive restaurant once and had seen what, for him, was the perfect example of how a true servant should behave. After seating them and serving their meal, the waiter stood at a distance with his napkin folded over his arm. He was far enough away that he could not overhear their conversation but close enough to quickly meet their every need. The waiter watched them carefully. Whenever their coffee cup or drinking glass was within a few sips of being empty, the waiter swiftly, but unobtrusively, moved to their table and refilled the cup or glass. He was ever watchful. They never had to ask for anything. If he saw even a puzzled look on their faces, he stepped closer and asked if he could be of service. Mel and his wife, Angela, felt they were truly being served.

Mel explained that first, this is the attitude we should have as servants of God. We should always be watching and waiting, ever sensitive to what God wants us to do. Then, we are to have this attitude toward those God has called us to serve. We should not have to be asked or told to do everything.

Although many of us may not have been to such an expensive restaurant and had our own personal waiter like Brother Mel, we have probably been to cheaper restaurants with far less attentive waiters. We know what it is like to have poor service. Many times I have looked and looked for the waiter to no avail. Sometimes I have even called as a waiter quickly rushed by only to have them ignore me. I have even embarrassed my children by getting up, going behind the counter and pouring myself another cup of coffee (while the waitress continued to talk, moony-eyed to her boyfriend, another waiter). This is not the kind of servant we are to be with our Lord or with each other.

Before Adam sinned, he and God walked together in the garden of Eden and enjoyed fellowship with one another. There was a change after Adam sinned.

Genesis 3:8-10, "And they heard the sound of the Lord God walking in the garden in the cool of the day, and the man and his wife hid themselves from the presence of the Lord God among

141

the trees of the garden.
9 Then the Lord God called to the man,
and said to him, 'Where are you?'
10 And he said, 'I heard the sound
of Thee in the garden, and I was
afraid because I was naked; so I hid
myself.'"

God now had to call for Adam. Adam no longer eagerly awaited the Lord's coming nor joined Him without being called. His new actions were a result of sin.

I believe we should respond immediately, just like in Ezekiel's vision of the four creatures and the wheels within the wheels. In describing the vision Ezekiel says:

Ezekiel 1:12, "And each went straight forward; wherever the spirit was about to go, they would go, without turning as they went."

Ezekiel 1:19-21, "And whenever the living beings moved, the wheels moved with them. And whenever the living beings rose from the earth, the wheels rose also.
20 Wherever the spirit was about to go, they would go in that direction. And the wheels rose close beside them; for the spirit of the living beings was in the wheels.
21 Whenever those went, these went;

**and whenever those stood still, these
stood still. And whenever those rose
from the earth, the wheels rose close
beside them; for the spirit of the living
beings was in the wheels."**

We have a picture of perfect unity and harmony.
There are no verbal commands and no discussion
about which way to go. Wherever and whenever the
spirit moved, the creatures moved and the wheels
moved. We are to be filled with the spirit of God.
Wherever He moves, we need to move.

Hebrews 13:8 says, "Jesus Christ is the same
yesterday and today, yes and forever." Jesus is our
example and He does not change. Therefore, Jesus
still has the attitude of a servant.

Principle 12:

People are the same everywhere.

Regardless of race, culture, or upbringing, people are all human beings. No matter how you dress them, no matter what they eat and no matter what language they speak, they still have the same sinful human nature. Therefore, the Bible applies to all people everywhere. The Bible is written to the human condition, not to just one group of chosen people.

I've ministered in Canada, India, Malaysia, The Philippines, Kenya and Japan as well as talking to brothers and sisters from all over the world. In our church in Shizuoka we have had people from Indonesia, Taiwan, Malaysia, The Philippines, India, Ghana, Nigeria, Russia, China, Iran, Australia, Poland, New Zealand, Singapore, Brazil, England, Scotland, and, obviously, the U.S. and Japan. Each culture has its own unique ways and customs, but the people and their problems are still the same. We have friends who moved to Mozambique and they have described the same problems we have here in Japan and back home in Alabama. The Bible speaks to all human problems and situations.

When I first came to Japan, I was asked to travel to the island of Borneo to spend two weeks with a tribe on the top of a mountain in Malaysia, just a few feet from the border of Indonesia. Graeme Fawcett, a New Zealander, had started a church on the top of this mountain in a village named Simuti. I've been there a total of three times now over the past 18 years.

145

There are about 200 people in the village. Presently 198 are confessing Christians. The last I heard there were only 2 people still holding out.

This sounds like an ideal community. There is only one church and everyone attends. I have been in meetings there when the Holy Spirit moved so wonderfully that almost the entire village was slain in the Spirit. Those who were not on the floor of the church were dancing and singing and praising God. It is a very special place.

However, when I talked to the local pastor he described many of the same problems I have in my local church in Japan. Neighbor still gets upset with neighbor. Some of the women in the church do not get along with other women. Some of the men still argue with other men about land boundaries and rights. People are people.

For all of its outward appearance, Japan is a very polite culture. My first three visits were for only two weeks each time. During those visits I was treated like royalty and never heard any one speak an unkind word. I was in for a rude awakening when I moved to Japan in 1985. After being here only a few months I was asked to sit in on a meeting between a Japanese pastor and two men who were attending his church. I was not prepared for what I witnessed.

Sitting by George Bostrom, the senior missionary I was working with, I did not understand what was being said but I certainly understood the facial expressions, gestures and vocal cues. The pastor was accused of misusing church funds. One of his accusers, a short, middle-aged man, stood up and began speaking in increasingly threatening tones. His face turned crimson as he took off his glasses and shook them in the face of the pastor. Watching him rant and wildly gesticulate, I turned to George and commented, "I'm very disappointed. They're just like Americans!"

Before moving to Japan, my wife and I spent ten years in a church we helped start and lead. Those ten years were some of the best and most difficult in our lives. Looking back, we can see that we were being trained in forming and maintaining relationships with special emphasis on conflict resolution. In the midst of that training I did not understand what God was preparing us for nor did I always count it all joy when people spoke ill of us. I was obviously a slow learner and had to repeat several courses. More than once I found myself in the same situations and with the same difficult people as God gave me opportunity after opportunity to learn His lesson. Now, I am grateful for all we experienced.

In the last 19 years in Japan, I have met, in Japanese form, every difficult person that I had to deal with in those ten years in that church. At times I have turned to my wife and said, "I know this person, he's just like Mr.___. We've met him before, just in an American body." Because of those prior experiences, I was not so badly shaken in encountering this personality or conflict in Japan. I had learned something from my training and was better prepared to face the situation this time.

At times my confidence in people has been shaken but my confidence in the validity and reliability of

God's Word has been strengthened again and again. I can go any where in the world and boldly teach the truths of the Bible because I know that those principles apply anywhere, any time, to any people. The Holy Spirit can apply God's truth in any culture or language. The Word is not bound by time, place, race, culture, or language. As brother A.S. Worley used to say, "Flesh is flesh." Unregenerate man is the same all over the world. Every human being needs to be born again and have his mind renewed. People are the same and God does not change.

Principle 13:

Don't fret too much over first reactions.

What people do in the end is more important than their first reactions. Jesus told the parable about the man who had two sons. One said he would go into the vineyard and work but did not go. The other said he would not go but later repented and went. Jesus emphasized that it was the second son who did his father's will.

> **Matthew 21:28-32, "But what do you think? A man had two sons, and he came to the first and said, 'Son, go work today in the vineyard.'**
> **29 And he answered and said, 'I will, sir'; and he did not go.**
> **30 And he came to the second and said the same thing. But he answered and said, 'I will not'; yet he afterward regretted it and went.**
> **31 Which of the two did the will of his father? They said, 'The latter.' Jesus said to them, 'Truly I say to you that the tax-gatherers and harlots will get into the kingdom of God before you.**
> **32 For John came to you in the way of righteousness and you did not believe him; but the tax-gatherers and harlots did believe him; and you, seeing this, did not even feel remorse afterward so as to believe him.'"**

149

The first response is often selfish, negative or based on fear. In Japan, the first answer is almost always, "NO." My wife is the director of Ai no Kesshin, (Loving Decisions in English) a non-profit, volunteer organization that helps women in crisis. Primarily we offer alternatives to abortion and help find homes for new-born-babies. My wife loves meeting and helping the mothers and babies. She really dislikes all the paperwork and confrontations with public officials who are often far less sympathetic to the plight of the mother and child. She has been told "NO!" so many times that she has learned not to react to that answer the first few times she hears it from a new official. She's learned that she has to help people work through their initial reaction to her request to do something new or different and help them find a way to give a positive response. Not reacting with an equal and opposite response, in other words, overriding her natural instinct, has allowed her to help many people trapped in unfortunate situations.

In the New Testament, Peter is a good example. Many of his first reactions were inappropriate or just plain wrong. It was Peter who spoke up and offered to build tabernacles to Moses, Elijah and Jesus on the mount of transfiguration.

Mark 9:2-7, "And six days later, Jesus took with Him Peter and James and John, and brought them up to a high mountain by themselves. And He was

150

transfigured before them;
3 and His garments became radiant
and exceedingly white, as no launderer
on earth can whiten them.
4 And Elijah appeared to them along with
Moses; and they were talking with Jesus.
5 And Peter answered and said to Jesus,
'Rabbi, it is good for us to be here; and let
us make three tabernacles, one for You,
and one for Moses, and one for Elijah.'
6 For he did not know what to answer;
for they became terrified.
7 Then a cloud formed, overshadowing them,
and a voice came out of the cloud, 'This is My
beloved Son, listen to Him!''

Peter spoke this out of great fear. The Father
responded by commanding him to listen to what the
Son had to say.

When Jesus explained to the twelve that he must
be betrayed and crucified, Peter rebuked him for
saying such things.

Matthew 16:21-23, "From that time
Jesus Christ began to show His disciples
that He must go to Jerusalem, and
suffer many things from the elders and
chief priests and scribes, and be killed,
and be raised up on the third day.
22 And Peter took Him aside and began
to rebuke Him, saying, 'God forbid it,
Lord! This shall never happen to You.'

151

23 But He turned and said to Peter, 'Get behind Me, Satan! You are a stumbling block to Me; for you are not setting your mind on God's interests, but man's. '"

Amplified Bible, v. 22, "...And began to reprove and charge Him sharply..."

Mark 8:33 Amp. Bible, v. 32, "...and Peter took Him by the hand and led Him aside, then [facing Him] began to rebuke Him."

Peter seems to take great liberty here with the man to whom he has just boldly confessed, "Thou art the Christ, the Son of the living God" (Matthew 16:16). Peter took Jesus by the hand, looked him right in the face and sharply rebuked his Messiah! Jesus gave his strongest rebuke to Peter on this occasion reminding him that his mind was not set on the interests of God but on the things of man.

When Jesus was giving a final explanation of what was to happen to Him and how they would respond Peter lead the others in swearing that he would never betray Christ, no matter what the other eleven did.

Mark 14:26-31, "And after singing a hymn, they went out to the Mount of Olives.
27 And Jesus said to them, 'You will all fall away, because it is written, 'I will strike down the shepherd, and the

sheep shall be scattered.'
28 But after I have been raised, I will
go before you to Galilee.
29 But Peter said to Him, 'Even though
all may fall away, yet I will not.'
30 And Jesus said to him, 'Truly I say to
you, that you yourself this very night,
before a cock crows twice, shall three
times deny Me.'
31 But Peter kept saying insistently,
'Even if I have to die with You, I will
not deny You!' And they all were saying
the same thing, too."

Luke adds a little extra to Peter's sworn allegiance to Christ. In Luke 22:33 Peter says, "Lord, with You I am ready to go both to prison and to death!" Peter's comparing himself to the others probably did not ingratiate himself to them.

When we read the story in Luke we see the great concern that Jesus had for Peter.

Luke 22:31-32, "Simon, Simon, behold,
Satan has demanded permission to sift
you like wheat;
32 but I have prayed for you, that your faith
may not fail; and you, when once you have
turned again, strengthen your brothers."

It is clear that Jesus knew Peter very well. He wanted Peter to understand himself much better. He tried to warn Peter that he was not as great as he thought he was but Peter kept right on insisting he would not deny Jesus. The Lord was just as faithful to Peter as he had been to King David when he had deceived himself about Bathsheba. Later David would declare in Psalms 51:6, "Behold, Thou dost desire truth in the innermost being, And in the hidden part Thou wilt make me know wisdom."

Again, in the passages in Mark and Luke we see that Jesus is telling the disciples what they will do before they get into the situation so that they will not be so shocked when it happens and so that they will not be so guilt ridden and condemned afterward.

The prophet Amos declared, "Surely the Lord God does nothing unless He reveals His secret counsel to His servants the prophets"[Amos 3:7]. God has always wanted to warn His people about serious events before they take place. Peter was continually warned about himself and upcoming events but would not listen.

When Judas and the soldiers came to arrest Jesus in the garden, it was Peter who drew his sword and cut off the ear of Malchus, servant of the high priest.

John 18:10-11, "Simon Peter therefore having a sword, drew it, and struck the high priest's slave, and cut off his right ear; and the slave's name was Malchus.
11 Jesus therefore said to Peter, "Put the sword into the sheath; the cup which the Father has given Me, shall I not drink it?"

This story is told in all four gospels. Only John mentions Peter's name and the name of the slave. Only Luke, the doctor, mentions that Jesus touched the man and healed his ear. Even at this crucial time in the life of Christ, Jesus had to correct Peter and heal the man Peter wounded.

Jesus did not fret too much over Peter's first reactions. He worked with Peter and showed him how to do better. He had faith in Peter from the beginning.

John 1:42, "He brought him to Jesus. Jesus looked at him, and said, "You are Simon the son of John; you shall be called Cephas" (which is translated Peter).

He changed Peter's name from Simon to Peter, *petros*, which means "rock, or stone." When Jesus met him, Peter was certainly not as stable as a rock, yet Christ was calling forth that which He knew Peter would become. When Peter confessed that Jesus was the Christ, the Son of God, Jesus used the meaning of Peter's name to declare a profound truth.

Matthew 16:18, "And I also say to you that you are Peter, and upon this rock I will build My church; and the gates of Hades shall not overpower it."

It was Peter who had the first real revelation that Jesus was the Messiah. Jesus told him, you are Peter, *petros*, a stone or smaller rock, and upon this rock,

155

.

petra, a massive rock, I will build my church. Jesus is the *Petra;* Peter is the *petros*. Jesus did not say this about any one else. He was giving Peter a place of honor, even though Peter was far from deserving this position by his previous actions and those that would soon follow.

After His resurrection, Jesus spent time restoring Peter in their conversation on the seashore.

John 21:15-17, "So when they had finished breakfast, Jesus said to Simon Peter, Simon, son of John, do you love Me more than these? He said to Him, 'Yes, Lord; You know that I love You.' He said to him, 'Tend My lambs.'
16 He said to him again a second time, 'Simon, son of John, do you love Me?' He said to Him, 'Yes, Lord; You know that I love You.' He said to him, 'Shepherd My sheep.'
17 He said to him the third time, 'Simon, son of John, do you love Me?' Peter was grieved because He said to him the third time, 'Do you love Me?' And he said to Him, 'Lord, You know all things; You know that I love You.' Jesus said to him, 'Tend My sheep.'"

I have heard different interpretations on why Jesus spoke the way He did to Peter. In Jesus' first two questions he uses the Greek word *agapao* for love while Peter answers every time using the Greek word *phileo* for love. Finally, Jesus uses *phileo* in his third question. *Agapao* is considered the higher form of love. It is used when the scriptures say "God is love " and is the word used in the definition of love in I Corinthians 13:4-8. *Agapao* is God's kind of love. It is unconditional, totally giving and sacrificing, unselfish and unending. *Phileo* has to do more with feelings of affection and love for a friend. It is sometimes called brotherly love.

I believe that in this simple conversation, Peter was getting another chance to be honest about himself. This time he demonstrated he really understood his true character. He made no pretense to have *agapao* like Jesus had demonstrated on the cross. He made it clear, with three answers in a row, that his love was not that great. On the last question, for the first time in their recorded conversations, Jesus and Peter are in agreement about "Peter." Peter is now ready to reestablish his identity in Christ. He will now stand on the solid rock (*petra*) of Christ, and build from there.

All Christ's input into Peter's life bore fruit on the day of Pentecost. On that crucial day, the birth of the church, it was Peter who stood and gave the first evangelistic sermon.

Acts 2:14, "But Peter, taking his stand with the eleven, raised his voice and declared to them: Men of Judea, and all you who live in Jerusalem, let this be known to you, and give heed to my words."

157

Acts 2:41, "So then, those who had received his word were baptized; and there were added that day about three thousand souls."

Three thousand people responded to that first sermon by the man whose first reactions had usually been wrong. Peter was the key and a rock of stability in founding the church at Jerusalem. Jesus did not hold his first reactions against him, even though so many were wrong. Again and again Jesus gave him the chance to change and get it right.

I saw an advertisement on a bus that read, "People don't remember how you came, just the way you leave." This seems to be God's attitude towards many people we read about in the Bible. When you read what God said about Old Testament people in the New Testament, you would think He had a faulty memory. Writing under the inspiration of the Holy Spirit, Peter refers to Abraham's nephew as "righteous Lot" who was tormented by the evils of Sodom and Gomorrah.

2 Peter 2:6-8, "And if He condemned the cities of Sodom and Gomorrah to destruction by reducing them to ashes, having made them an example to those who would live ungodly thereafter;
7 and if He rescued righteous Lot, oppressed by the sensual conduct of unprincipled men
8 (for by what he saw and heard that

righteous man, while living among them, felt his righteous soul tormented day after day with their lawless deeds.)"

I look at Lot in Genesis and I don't particularly see a righteous man. I see a man who made many bad decisions. He chose to settle in Sodom and Gomorrah. He led his family to dwell in the midst of unparalleled decadence. It was probably the influence of living in Sodom that led to his wife's death and his daughters' decision to seduce him and bear his children. Yet, God refers to him as a righteous man.

There was no disciple more understanding than Peter to write these words about Lot. Who else could write with such compassion about a man who had made so many bad choices? The Holy Spirit, writing through Peter, could convey the tremendous mercy and grace of God better than through any other of the original twelve.

One of the cultural quirks of Japan is that people often do not get a second chance. This is a very unforgiving culture. After three years in Shizuoka, our church and family had out grown the home where we had started. We found an empty place on the other side of town that was just right. The first floor had been a dental supply office and the owner's family lived on the second and third floors. The new owner, a real estate agent in Tokyo, was eager to rent because the building had been vacant for over a year. After we moved in and met the neighbors we learned the sad story behind our new home.

The neighbors awakened one morning to

find the building suddenly empty and the family gone. Without saying goodbye to anyone in the neighborhood or giving any explanation or warning, the business and the family disappeared. A short time later, *yakuza* (Japanese organized crime figures) starting coming around asking questions about the former occupants and taking anything of value that remained in the office area. Neighbors learned later that the original owner had borrowed heavily from loan sharks and was unable to pay. This explained part of the clandestine evacuation of the premises.

However, the unforgiving character of the Japanese neighbors explains the other part. If the business had failed or if the *yakuza* had come around with the family still living there, the family would never be able to outlive the shame. No one would forget, or let them forget, what had happened. They would be forever tainted in the eyes of the neighborhood. The only second chance they could get would be in a new place where no one knew them.

One reason the house had remained empty so long was because people feared there was a curse on the property. After our family and church occupied the house and prospered there, it was probably much easier to rent when we departed.

We have heard many similar stories about people leaving in the middle of the night to escape an unforgiving neighborhood. We even heard of one deacon who dropped by the pastor's house one Saturday morning only to find it completely empty. We never heard what happened that caused the pastor to flee. Obviously he felt there was no second chance in his church.

One of the unique attributes of Christianity is the forgiveness we receive through Christ. Jesus offers a new start, a second or third or fourth chance to those whose first responses were wrong and destructive. In Christ, you can start over. It is no accident that Peter is such a central character in the gospel story and in the history of the first church. There are Peters in every culture who need to know that their sins can be forgiven, start again and become all that God intended them to be.

Principle 14:

There is always a solution.

The problem, as stated by people, may not be solvable. Praise God, people are not the final authority on anything! "He will always...provide the way out."

Proverbs 3:5-8, "Trust in the Lord with all your heart, And do not lean on your own understanding.
6 In all your ways acknowledge Him, And He will make your paths straight.
7 Do not be wise in your own eyes; Fear the Lord and turn away from evil.
8 It will be healing to your body, And refreshment to your bones."

1 Corinthians 10:13, "No temptation has overtaken you but such as is common to man; and God is faithful, who will not allow you to be tempted beyond what you are able, but with the temptation will provide the way of escape also, that you may be able to endure it.
Amplified Bible, "...He [can be trusted] not to let you be tempted and tried and assayed beyond your ability and strength of resistance and power to endure, but with the temptation He

163

**will [always] also provide the way out--
the means of escape to a landing place--
that you may be capable and strong and
powerful patiently to bear up under it."**

Remember that with God all things are possible.
Let me cite three references just to confirm that the
Word does teach this.

[1] The Angel Gabriel to Mary when
explaining how she can conceive:
**Luke 1:37, "For nothing will be
impossible with God."**

[2] Jesus speaking to the twelve disciples;
**Matthew 19:26, "And looking upon
them Jesus said to them, "With
men this is impossible, but with
God all things are possible."**

[3] Jesus speaking to the father of a
demon possessed son:
**Mark 9:2, "And Jesus said to him,
If You can! All things are possible
to him who believes."**

Nothing is impossible with God. It does not matter
how many experts agree. God is the final word.

My grandfather Gordon, "D", loved telling me
one story over and over. He relished saying, "You
know, I've had six doctors tell me that I was going to
die. I buried them all!" When he finished, he'd throw

back his head and laugh loudly.

"D" was so over weight and had so many additional contributing problems that six doctors during his life had said, at one time or another, there was nothing they could do to save him. Across a span of fifty years they all agreed, "You are going to die." What they did not understand was that "D" had a living relationship with God, whom he called "The Master." "D" was convinced he was not going to die until "The Master" was ready for him to die. As a result, "D" always recovered and eventually he attended the funeral of each of those six doctors. When he finally died at the age of 84, my grandfather was ready to go home. He died in peace, knowing it was "The Master's" time, not the doctor's time. Every time the doctors said, "There is no solution," God had His own answer, His own way.

When I first started teaching college in Decatur, Alabama, I had several local policemen take my public speaking class. I enjoyed talking to them after class because I had never personally known any policemen. During one conversation they asked me, "Do you know which distress call we hate to answer most?" My first thoughts were of bank robberies or shoot outs between gangs or something of a similar nature. All my answers were wrong.

"The phone call we dread the most is from a woman who is fighting with her husband. This is the most dangerous call we respond to."

I was shocked and of course asked, "Why?"

"Because we can't win in a family fight," they explained. "Too often the wife wants her husband locked up, but when she sees him handcuffed, she suddenly feels sorry for him. Then she turns on us. Sometimes we are in greater danger from the suddenly loving wife than we were from the fighting husband. We can't win in a situation like that."

His comment that "we can't win in a family fight" often appears to be true. It has always fascinated me how Jesus responded to a very delicate family dilemma. Reading the following description in context, my impression is that Jesus is teaching the people many things when a man in the crowd suddenly blurts out this request.

> **Luke 12:13-16, "And someone in the crowd said to Him, 'Teacher, tell my brother to divide the family inheritance with me.'**
> **14 But He said to him, 'Man, who appointed Me a judge or arbiter over you?'**
> **15 And He said to them, 'Beware, and be on your guard against every form of greed; for not even when one has an abundance does his life consist of his possessions. '**
> **16 And He told them a parable, saying ..."**

Jesus' response seems almost inappropriate or, at least, uncaring. Jesus refused to get involved in what would have been a no-win situation, at least for Jesus. Rather than say who was right or wrong, Jesus confronted the underlying motives that caused the conflict. In this case, greed was the underlying root of the family conflict. So, Jesus refuses to be the judge. Instead, he warns of the dangers of "greed" and uses this as an opportunity to teach the multitude through the parable that followed.

If you have enough close relationships you will one day find yourself in a similar situation. To you, everyone may seem right (or wrong) yet you are asked to be the judge. No matter what you decide, you will make someone unhappy. Many years ago I found myself in just such a situation.

I was asked to settle a dispute between two ladies in our church. One was a middle-aged school teacher named Frieda. She and the much younger woman, June, had argued and argued over an issue. Finally, they asked me to act as arbitrator. I don't remember the nature of the disagreement. I only remember that as I listened to them, both sounded right. This was not one of those issues where one person is clearly violating the Word of God and the other is not. As so many of these disputes are, it was simply a matter of personal evaluation with two very different people seeing the same situation from very different points of view.

After each presented her side, it was obvious neither was going to change. Each equally believed she was right and the other was wrong. I felt that nothing I could say would persuade either of them. It is one of the situations I hate most. I hate that feeling of helplessness—that feeling that no matter what I do, it will not affect the outcome of the confrontation. I looked at both of them sitting quietly but very stiffly. Not knowing what to say or do, I suggested we pray.

I prayed some "pastorly type prayer" for wisdom and healing but I wasn't concentrating on what I said. In my mind I was begging God to do something, anything. In just a few minutes, Frieda quietly stood up and left the room. I felt even more helpless. June and I just sat there with our eyes closed and heads bowed.

As quietly as she left, Frieda slipped back into the room. She had a plastic bowl of water and a towel. Frieda knelt on the floor before June and slowly removed the younger woman's shoes. June's body was more rigid than ever. I watched Frieda gently and silently wash one foot and then the other. Before her feet were dried, June softened and broke into sobs. She and Frieda held each other and cried as the Holy Spirit healed their hearts and restored their relationship.

Words and reasoning would never have brought brokenness and healing. I could have ordered the younger to submit to the elder and June may have submitted. That would not have really satisfied either of them. The issue of who was really right and who was really wrong would have remained. When one humbled herself and served the other though, both hearts were softened and a, heretofore unseen way for restoration, was opened. By this way, the issue of right and wrong no longer mattered. Love prevailed over rights.

I am convinced that there is always a solution if we will only seek God's wisdom. God desires to lead us away from so many deadlocks that our pride and fear lead us into. If we will only seek Him enough, and be willing to do what He says, then a solution is available that will usually bless both parties. I saw the need for both these components, seeking His wisdom and being willing to obey, in a young high school student in Japan.

Toshiro lived in the first neighborhood we were in as missionaries in Japan. I taught him English after the New Zealander who had led him to the Lord moved away. Toshiro was a very sensitive, serious student. When he became a Christian, he was as committed to the Lord as he was to his studies. He was the youngest of three in his family. His parents were delighted that his goal was to become a doctor. Being a good Japanese mother, his mother insisted he study with the diligence necessary to pass the very difficult and competitive entrance exams for medical universities.

The conflict arose as church attendance conflicted with studies. I remember Toshiro coming to me with his problem. As a Christian, he wanted to obey his mother. He knew he must demonstrate Christian obedience to his unsaved parents. However, Toshiro knew that he needed teaching and fellowship and that he could not survive without going to church. His mother felt like he could not study enough and still go to church on Sunday morning. He asked me for guidance.

We discussed both sides of the issue. We had scriptures for both positions. I did not feel I could tell him to disobey his mother nor could I tell him to abandon church for a year. The best I could say was, "Toshiro, I know there is a solution that will please

169

you, your mother and God. Pray that God will give you His wisdom and His solution. I can't tell you what to do. I'll pray for you, but you have to seek the Lord yourself." I knew he was serious enough about his walk to do that.

We did not talk about it for some time. Toshiro did not miss church nor did he mention any more conflict with his mother. At some point I remembered to ask him what had happened. Toshiro had found a solution that would allow him to continue attending church and that pleased his mother. On Saturday night he would study until 12:00 or 1:00 A.M. He would sleep for three or four hours, then get up again around 4:00 A.M. and study until it was time to go to church. As soon as he returned from church, he would study again until bedtime. At great cost to his personal comfort, he had found a way to obey both God and his mother.

I was very humbled when I heard Toshiro's solution. Too often I have complained to God that there is no solution. In reality I have to admit that there were solutions God had given. It is simply that I haven't been willing to sacrifice my own desires, my own comfort, to implement those solutions. If we will seek His wisdom and then execute His plan, we will be blessed and become a blessing to others.

Toshiro passed the entrance exam for two medical universities. He chose the one closer to home so he could continue to bless his parents and stay in church. He is now married to the pastor's daughter and finishing up a specialty in pathology. He and his wife just started a new church in their home. God's solution continues to add blessings to his life and to many others.

I am convinced by the Word and by experience that there is always a solution to every problem. With us, many things are impossible; but, with God, all things are possible! When we seek God's Wisdom, He promises that we will, "discern righteousness and justice and equity and **every good course**" (Proverbs 2:9). [Bold print added by author.]

Principle 15:

You cannot be both inclusive and exclusive at the same time.

Jesus said, "He who is not with Me is against Me; and he who does not gather with Me scatters"[Matthew 12:30]. Paul wrote to both the Ephesians and the Colossians making it clear that you are either in the kingdom of light or in the kingdom of darkness.

Ephesians 5:8, "For you were formerly darkness, but now you are light in the Lord; walk as children of light."

Colossians 1:13, "For He delivered us from the domain of darkness, and transferred us to the kingdom of His beloved Son."

When warning about the coming of the Antichrist and those with his same spirit, John also explained about some of the people who had left them.

1 John 2:18-19, "Children, it is the last hour; and just as you heard that antichrist is coming, even now many antichrists have arisen; from this we know that it is the last hour.
19 They went out from us, but they were not really of us; for if they had been of us, they would have remained

with us; but they went out, in order that it might be shown that they all are not of us."

The letter of Jude also warns about those who seem to be part of the church, the family of God, and yet they are not.

Jude 1:12-13,16, "These men are those who are hidden reefs in your love feasts when they feast with you without fear, caring for themselves; clouds without water, carried along by winds; autumn trees without fruit, doubly dead, uprooted;
13 wild waves of the sea, casting up their own shame like foam; wandering stars, for whom the black darkness has been reserved forever...
16 These are grumblers, finding fault, following after their own lusts; they speak arrogantly, flattering people for the sake of gaining an advantage."

Selfishness is a hallmark of these people. They care only for themselves and only compliment others to gain an advantage. They also find fault and complain unceasingly.

My point though is that you are either with Christ or against Him. You are either in or out. You are either in the family of God or you are outside the family of God. You are either included or excluded.

The choice is yours.

Once you make the choice to be in, you must have the same attitude that Christ has. All those who are accepted by Jesus must be willing to accept all others that Christ accepts. We are no longer allowed the foolishness of cliques that the world loves to create. These little groups tend to exclude those not deemed fitting. This goes against the very heart of Christ. God is not willing that any should perish [2 Peter 3:9]. Jesus came because God loves the whole world, not just a chosen few. When they receive Jesus, the Holy Spirit does His work. "For by one Spirit are we all baptized into one body, whether we be Jews or Gentiles, whether we be bond or free; and have been all made to drink into one Spirit" [1 Corinthians 12:13]. We are included in the "one body." We cannot exclude those who are already included in the Body of Christ, the Family of God.

In too many churches I have noticed people who want to be included in all things but they also want to exclude those who they expect to include them. This seems to show up most frequently in personal relationships within the body. One person insists that they must be included in everything that the church or one certian person does. If they are not invited or included, they feel very rejected and hurt. However, they always reserve the right to say "no" and often keep many things private so that they may include only special people in their plans. The problem is if you exclude someone from your life, you cannot expect them to include you in theirs. You cannot be both inclusive and exclusive at the same time.

A young woman complained to me that two other women were not including her in their lives. They were all friends but the young woman complained that her two friends talked very openly and intimately with one another but did not open up with her. She also felt slighted that they occasionally gave special gifts to each other but did not do such nice things for her. I listened patiently as I recalled comments the other two women had made about her over several years. They had told me how this young woman excluded them again and again from activities they would have all enjoyed together. They had told me how the young woman, who now felt so left out, would frequently make no comments about herself when they shared and how she would just get up in the middle of a discussion or game and leave without a word. She had sown a pattern of exclusion and rejection that she was now reaping; yet, she had no idea why her two friends were not open with her. After all, she was now ready to be open and included. She had felt free for years to exclude her two friends from her personal life.

You cannot live in separate worlds without causing great harm to both. You cannot live with one foot in the kingdom of darkness and the other in the kingdom of light. You cannot serve both God and mammon. You cannot love the world and love God with all your heart. Nor can you love and include part of the body of Christ in your life while choosing to exclude other parts that are not to your liking or up to your standards.

I seem to meet more people who cannot manage

more than one good relationship at a time. They can only be someone's best friend for a season. They are not able to share that friend with anyone else. They become possessive as they always include the new friend but seek to exclude others. In the end, they will leave the new best friend and move on to another new best friend. The one left behind is often shattered by the experience.

We all want to be special. We all need special attention sometimes. However, we must never seek to exclude other members of the body of Christ from our lives. Our goal is to always promote unity and those actions that create and maintain unity.

Principle 16:

Silence is not golden.

In relationships silence leads to confusion, distrust and deceit. It is vitally important that we communicate and not remain silent. We know that to exercise faith we must speak what we believe. Speaking what we believe is vital to our salvation, our relationship with God and our walk in faith. **Romans 10:8-13 says,**

> **8 "But what does it say? The word is near you, in your mouth and in your heart-- that is, the word of faith which we are preaching,**
> **9 that if you confess with your mouth Jesus as Lord, and believe in your heart that God raised Him from the dead, you shall be saved;**
> **10 for with the heart man believes, resulting in righteousness, and with the mouth he confesses, resulting in salvation.**
> **11 For the Scripture says, 'Whoever believes in Him will not be disappointed.'**
> **12 For there is no distinction between Jew and Greek; for the same Lord is Lord of all, abounding in riches for all who call upon Him;**
> **13 for 'Whoever will call upon the name of the Lord will be saved. '"**

We must believe in our hearts and confess with our mouths "...the word is nigh thee, in your mouth...." It is not enough to believe in your heart but you must also confess with your mouth. We call upon the name of the Lord with our mouth. We must verbalize the desire and belief in our heart to receive salvation from the Lord.

In Matthew and Mark, "ye shall have what you say...."

Matthew 17:20, "And He said to them, Because of the littleness of your faith; for truly I say to you, if you have faith as a mustard seed, <u>you shall say to this mountain</u>, 'Move from here to there,' and it shall move; and nothing shall be impossible to you."

[Underline added by author.]

Mark 11:22-24, "And Jesus answered saying to them, Have faith in God.
23 Truly I say to you, <u>whoever says to this mountain</u>, 'Be taken up and cast into the sea,' and does not doubt in his heart, but believes that what he says is going to happen, it shall be granted him.
24 Therefore I say to you, all things for which you pray and ask, believe that you have received them, and they shall be granted you."

[Underline added by author.]

Isaiah 57:19 (KJV), "<u>I create the fruit of the lips</u>; Peace, peace to him that is far off, and to him that is near, saith the LORD; and I will heal him."

[Underline added by author.]

In Jesus' parable about the wedding feast, the improperly clothed guest did not say anything when asked by the king why he was not wearing the wedding garments provided. He was cast into the outer darkness.

Matthew 22:11-14, "But when the king came in to look over the dinner guests, he saw there a man not dressed in wedding clothes,
12 and he said to him, 'Friend, how did you come in here without wedding clothes?' And <u>he was speechless</u>.
13 Then the king said to the servants, 'Bind him hand and foot, and cast him into the outer darkness; in that place there shall be weeping and gnashing of teeth.'
14 For many are called, but few are chosen." *[Underline added by author.]*

He was cast out because he did not have on the proper clothing that had been provided. When asked for an explanation, he said nothing. Might he have received grace to still put on the appropriate attire if he had given some reasonable explanation? We don't know for sure. Since he said nothing, the king dealt severely with him.

We are told, "Be angry, and yet do not sin; do not let the sun go down on your anger," (Ephesians 4:26). In other words, don't go to sleep without settling the issue. Don't say, "Let's sleep on it," and refuse to talk.

Paul instructs the Romans, "If possible, so far as it depends on you, be at peace with all men" (Romans 12:18).

Jesus said,

Matthew 5:23-24, "If therefore you are presenting your offering at the altar, and there remember that your brother has something against you,
24 leave your offering there before the altar, and go your way; first be reconciled to your brother, and then come and present your offering."

Almost 100% of the time this reconciliation requires us to open our mouths and say something. We must believe and speak to be reconciled to God and to our fellow man. Too many people, all over the world, want to believe that they can just ignore a problem and pretend like nothing was said or done and everything will be alright in time. Contrary to popular belief, time does not heal all wounds. We are commanded to be reconciled to God and to one another. Silence is not a great healer.

After the death of my father, my mother remarried when I was 5 years old. My step-father, who I called "Daddy Blount," was the "strong, silent type." All my growing up years I never remember Daddy Blount saying, "I love you," or, "I'm sorry." Whenever he and my mother had an argument, he would get in his truck and drive off. He would come back a few minutes or hours later and act like nothing ever happened. This was his pattern for over forty years.

After his death, I asked my mother how they had worked through problems in their marriage. She said they really didn't. He would always leave and come back later. He would never talk about what had happened. She said she could tell when he was sorry because he would always be very nice later. As his wife, she was never satisfied with that behavior. She never felt they settled the disagreements. She always wanted him to talk things out, but he was either unwilling or unable to verbally communicate.

I wasn't there when Daddy Blount died. Later I asked my mother, "Did he open up and talk at the end? Did he ever really pour out his heart to you?" "No," she said. "He died just like he lived." There were years of unresolved issues between them that never were talked out and put to rest. She had to make her peace without the comfort of hearing him say so many words she had longed for over forty years of marriage.

I know that Jesus kept silent before Pilate and said almost nothing before the Sanhedrin; but, these were not people in relationship with Jesus nor were these normal circumstances. And yes, even a fool is thought to be wise when he keeps his mouth shut but we are instructed repeatedly not to be fools. Jesus did talk to the masses; he talked even more to his 12 disciples, explaining what he did not explain to the masses; and he talked even more intimately with his three closest disciples, Peter, James and John. After His resurrection, He even went to great pains to heal Peter as He talked with him after breakfast on the sea shore. He did not just leave Peter guessing whether he was loved and forgiven. He took the time to verbally communicate His love and acceptance to one who had betrayed both Him and his [Peter's] own convictions.

Silence is not golden in the relationships God gives us. As a pastor, I don't want anyone to leave my church. I realize that, at times, people will leave and that sometimes God is moving them to another church. I can accept that, even though I will greatly miss them. What hurts the most is when friends leave the church with no explanation at all.

Probably the most painful event in my families early years in Japan was the way James left our church. He had been with us for about five years. James was a very faithful church member. He was on the worship team and even shared occasionally on Sundays when I was out of town. The worship team met at our house every week so he was always there and often came early or stayed later than the others. Every Sunday night he would come by to fellowship and watch videos with the family. Our children loved him just like a big brother.

When James got married we were all surprised but happy for him. It soon became clear that James' wife was not very happy in our church. Part of the problem was doctrinal but part of the problem also seemed to be the need to establish her identity in a place where her husband was already settled and loved. Looking back we can see the signs of what was coming but we were still unprepared for the way they departed. James made a business trip back to his home country and his wife joined him. This took them away from the church for over six weeks. When James returned, his wife stayed behind a little longer visiting family and friends.

When James did not come to church after his return, I stopped by his office to welcome him back and see if he was alright. Without looking at me, James informed me that he and his wife were looking for another church. He gave no explanation. I asked if he would like to come back to church and say goodbye to everyone. I thought it would be good for him, and the church, if he would give at least a brief farewell speech. He said no. Sitting across from him at his desk, I realized he wasn't going to tell me anything else either. I finally said, "Look, James, you can't just leave without telling me something. If you won't say anything to the church, I have to. You've been with us for five years and been up front every Sunday helping lead worship. I have to give some kind of explanation."

He gave me a few reasons about how the church had changed since he joined. He had doctrinal issues about what had been happening in the church as a result of the recent moves of the Holy Spirit among us and particularly the physical manifestations of people falling on the floor. We didn't talk much and that was the end.

I saw James many times after he left the church because we were involved in certain business activities together. From that day in his office, he never mentioned my family or the church again. Every conversation we had was business only, nothing personal. He never called nor came by my house again. For my wife and children, it was the same as a family member suddenly dying. It took years to get over the pain of that loss. My small children would ask me, "Why doesn't James come any more? He doesn't like us?" My wife and older children were deeply wounded by the total rejection of someone they had thought was a very close friend. I fluctuated between anger and sorrow and had to forgive James again and again. For years, every time I had to work with him I would feel the pangs of rejection.

The fact that James left the church and severed his relationship with our family probably was unavoidable. If he had talked to the people in the church, they would have gotten over his departure much quicker. If he had just said anything to my family, they would have been able to overcome the pain of his leaving much sooner. The greatest pain was in "how" he left.

As in so many cases, silence is interpreted as rejection. Receiving the silent treatment from those who are fully capable of communicating not only wounds deeply, it can cause physical illness and even death to those on the receiving end. In England years ago, there was a punishment referred to as "sent to

Coventry." It was similar to a severe punishment inflicted on those who had offended the tribal community in some primitive cultures. To send a child (or a tribal member) "to Coventry" meant that the other members of the family ignored the child as though he did not exist. In later years, some British children said they would rather have been badly thrashed than to be treated like they were invisible. In some tribes, the group identity is so strong that such treatment eventually resulted in the ostracized member wandering off into the jungle or bush and dying. Silence can be deadly! It certainly does not promote healing in most cases.

Principle 17:

Seeds are accurate indicators of the crop to be harvested.

If you see the seed you'll know in advance what the crop will be. If you see a farmer planting corn, you don't have to wait 3 months or longer to know what the harvest will bring. It is God's pattern from the beginning. If you plant corn you will pick corn from the plants later.

Jesus said that we would know men by their fruits. This is certainly true and I will discuss it further in Principle 18. Many times we must patiently wait to see what fruit will come from certain actions and words. However, it is also true that certain actions spoken of in the Bible will produce certain results. For example, Proverbs 11:29 says, "He who troubles his own house will inherit wind..." Trouble here means "to stir up, disturb, to trouble." If you see a man continually disturbing his house, his family, we know that he is going to "inherit wind." We can interpret this to mean that he is going to inherit nothing, just like wind; or, it may mean something much stronger.

The word for wind is *ruach*, the Hebrew word signifying a very strong desert wind, the kind that splits the rocks and blows up dust storms. When Elijah was running from Jezebel and God confronts him about his behavior, God sends a *ruach*, wind.

1 Kings 19:11, "So He said, Go forth, and stand on

the mountain before the Lord. And behold, the Lord was passing by! And a great and strong wind [*ruach*] was rending the mountains and breaking in pieces the rocks before the Lord..."

Ruach is a powerful, forceful wind that can be very destructive. It was the *ruach* that brought in the locusts to plague Egypt at Moses' command. It was the *ruach* that parted the Red Sea for the children of Israel to cross over and it was the *ruach* that caused the waters to drown the Egyptian army. To inherit *ruach* could mean to inherit destruction.

In both Ephesians and Colossians there is a warning to men about how they should relate to their wife and their children. Colossians 3:19, 21 are particularly clear in the Amplified Bible.

Colossians 3:19, 21 (Amplified Bible), "Husbands, love your wives—be affectionate and sympathetic with them—and do not be harsh or bitter or resentful toward them...Fathers, do not provoke or irritate or fret your children—do not be hard on them or harass them; lest they become discouraged and sullen and morose and feel inferior and frustrated; do not break their spirit."

If you see a man verbally or physically abusing his wife and children you don't have to wait fifteen or twenty years to know that there will be many problems in the family. Fathers who provoke and irritate their children or harass them will make their children discouraged and create feelings of inferiority and frustration. Therefore when we see these seeds being sown into young lives we need to speak to the father about what he is planting in his children.

The passage we referred to in Proverbs 24:30-34 is another example. The writer talks about passing by the field of the sluggard. He observes and learns that if a man is lazy and does not work his field, it will be overgrown with weeds. It will not produce a crop and poverty will ensue. Paul instructed in the New Testament that, "If a man will not work, neither let him eat" (2 Thessalonians 3:10). We don't have to wait a long time to see what will happen to a lazy person who refuses to work. Rather, we are told to warn and admonish those people. We see them sowing seeds of poverty and should warn them in advance of the consequences of their deeds, or rather, their lack of deeds. When you see bad seeds going in the ground, you don't have to wait to know a bad crop will be harvested.

Practically speaking, we can readily see what seeds we are sowing with our own bodies. If we live on fast food and junk food, never exercise and live a stressful life, we know that we are sowing the seeds of our own physical destruction. Although Paul wrote Timothy that, "...bodily exercise profiteth little: but godliness is profitable unto all things, having promise of the life that now is, and of that which is to come," (1 Timothy 4:8, KJV), he also wrote the Corinthians reminding them that "...your body is a temple of the

Holy Spirit who is in you, whom you have from God, and that you are not your own. For you have been bought with a price: therefore glorify God in your body"
(1 Corinthians 6:19-20).

Principle 18:

Whatever you sow, you will reap.

Galatians 6:7 (Amplified Bible), "Do not be deceived and deluded and misled; God will not allow Himself to be sneered at—scorned, disdained or mocked [by mere pretensions or professions, or His precepts being set aside]—He inevitably deludes himself who attempts to delude God. For whatever a man sows, that and that only is what he will reap. For he who sows to his own flesh (lower nature, sensuality) will from the flesh reap decay and ruin and destruction; but he who sows to the Spirit reap life eternal."

In no other place is sowing and reaping more relevant or evident than in our relationships. The scriptures above are very strong and emphatic about this principle. In some cases we can detect the seeds that are being sown and seek to replace those bad seeds with good ones. In other instances, we are not able to detect what is being sown and must therefore evaluate the fruit that is being produced. Seeing the good fruit, we may judge that good seeds were sown. Seeing bad fruit, we must now work backwards to determine what went wrong.

As I mentioned in Principle 8, children are very sensitive to others. They are feelers and as a result respond very quickly to what they perceive. Watching a child respond to a stranger they meet for the first time can be most enlightening. I have had many guests from many different countries in my home over the years and have marveled to see the varied responses my young children have given. I am happy to report that the vast majority of our guests have received warm welcomes from our little ones.

However, that has not been true 100% of the time. It is particularly those exceptions that I have learned to scrutinize closely. Almost every time that my children have not responded well to someone I have later had problems with those people myself. I have learned that I make many exceptions and overlook small things in an effort to be gracious, but my children have not yet learned to do that. Instead, they respond almost immediately when someone is filled with insecurity or rejection or condemnation. They feel what is coming out of the person in some little tone of voice or facial expression or gesture and they respond accordingly. They instinctively sense what is being sown. I am not so sensitive to such things.

Sowing and reaping is a Biblical principle that runs throughout the Bible. The scripture above is very emphatic, "For whatever a man sows, that and that only is what he will reap." If we sow to the flesh, we reap from the flesh and that will lead to decay and destruction and death. If we sow to the Spirit, we reap from the Spirit that leads to growth, blessing and life.

Without a doubt the most significant examples of sowing and reaping I have witnessed in my life came through the living testimony of my Uncle Olin. When

194

I was nine years old, I started working on Saturday afternoons at Smith's Grocery, a small country store that sold everything from food to chicken feed to clothes to gasoline. Uncle Olin sold all the basic necessities of life.

He was exceedingly generous and frequently gave people food on credit, knowing that probably he would never be repaid in full. His motto was, "The customer is always right" and he tried to meet everyone's need as quickly as possible—with a smile.

I remember my aunt getting quite frustrated with his generosity. Again and again, I remember her saying, "Olin, you're going to give away everything we've got. When we get old we won't have a thing!"

After forty plus years Uncle Olin had to close Smith's Grocery. When he did, he closed the books on a large stack of unpaid debts. I don't know if he even knows how much money people never paid. I never heard him complain or even comment about it. My aunt passed away suddenly when Uncle Olin was about seventy years old. That was about 14 years ago.

I've been watching my uncle closely to see if he really "gave away everything he had" and doesn't "have anything now." The fact is, Uncle Olin is in his early eighties now and has more than he has ever had in his life! For over forty years he sowed to the Lord by giving to those in need. Sure, he probably sowed a lot into bad soil that would never produce anything except thorns. But, apparently, Jesus did, too. In His parable of the sower, the man sowing only has 25% of his precious seed land on good soil. That means 75% produced nothing of lasting value. And yet, that

25% that did land on good soil was capable of bringing forth a 30 or 40 or 100 fold return!

My aunt may have been right that Uncle Olin gave away a lot of goods that he shouldn't have; but, he hit enough good ground that God has met all of his needs ever since. Let me give you a recent example.

A few years ago parts of the southern United States experienced a severe drought. Uncle Olin has always kept twenty-five to fifty head of cows on his farm. That year there was just not enough rain in south Alabama for the grass to grow. The result was a drastic shortage of hay for the cows to eat during the winter. Even if there had been hay to buy Uncle Olin did not have the money to buy more. He didn't know what he could do.

Speaking through the prophet Isaiah, God promised, "And it shall come to pass, that before they call, I will answer; and while they are yet speaking, I will hear" (Isaiah 65:24). Before Uncle Olin called, God had already prepared the answer. The farmers of north Alabama had received an abundance of rain that year. They offered to give their extra hay to the cattle farmers of south Alabama if they could find a way to get it to them. Truckers heard about the offer and agreed to haul the hay to the south when they were making return trips with empty trucks. This hay met most but not all of Uncle Olin's need for winter hay.

A short time later he was visiting the church graveyard to make sure all was well with the grounds and noticed that a field near the graveyard had uncut hay. Having known the owner of the field for years, he called to ask if he could buy some of the hay. The elderly man said that he didn't need the hay and was unable to cut it himself but that if Uncle Olin would cut his field he could have all the hay he wanted. This supplied the rest of the winter feed necessary to take care of his cows. I wish my aunt could have lived to see, and come to understand, the blessing of sowing abundantly and the abundant harvest that comes. We need to commit to memory the words of Paul to the Galatians.

Galatians 6:9-10, "And let us not lose heart in doing good, for in due time we shall reap if we do not grow weary.
10 So then, while we have opportunity, let us do good to all men, and especially to those who are of the household of the faith."

Before we leave this subject of sowing and reaping, let me mention a corollary principle. When Jesus journeyed with his disciples through Sychar in Samaria he explained to them that **sometimes you reap where you have not sown**. He said:

John 4:37-38, "For in this case the saying is true, 'One sows, and another reaps.'
38 "I sent you to reap that for which you have not labored; others have labored, and you have entered into their labor."

Jesus is about to reap a city-wide harvest in Samaria yet neither he nor his disciples had ever gone there.

They are going to reap from another's labors. This frequently happens when we have the opportunity to lead someone to new birth in Christ. What we are reaping, the salvation of that person, is often the result of many people sowing an abundance of seeds over a long period of time. We are just fortunate to reap where others have sown.

When it comes to our sowing with a view to reaping, particularly in the area of finances, we also need to apply this truth. In the midst of a very traumatic experience early in my marriage my wife and I learned this principle: "Don't look to reap from the same place you have sown. Sow unto the Lord and trust him to provide whenever and by whomever He pleases." God was preparing us for future ministry and this was one of the many principles we needed to learn.

About three weeks before I received my master's degree and my wife and I moved to a different town to start new jobs, our apartment caught on fire. We didn't lose very many things to the fire but we had extensive smoke damage. If you have never stood in the midst of a place that has been filled with acrid smoke, you cannot fully appreciate the feeling of despair that overwhelms you. I arrived at the apartment only minutes before my wife. Most of our albums, our TV and all our Tupperware had melted. Everything in the apartment would have to be cleaned or thrown away.

Before we could sink into despair, church people began to arrive. Some began wiping down furniture while others took arms full of clothes to the cleaners or home to be washed. We were never without support in those crucial first few hours. One of my professors, who was also an elder in our church, told us we could live in his house for the next three weeks until we had to move. All our immediate needs for comfort and encouragement were met by our brothers and sisters from Auburn Christian Fellowship.

In the next few days we were able to assess our loss and calculate how many items would have to be replaced. We had not figured these new expenses into our moving budget. When I added up the numbers, I had a growing sense that God would provide all the money we needed. I was certain that, since the church had been so supportive, one of the leaders would give us a check to cover our losses. I was excited to go to church the next Sunday because I just knew that someone would walk up to me and say, "Here, this is to help replace all you lost," and give me a sizeable check.

I smiled at everyone we met that morning and thanked all those who had washed and cleaned and brought us food. I waited and waited for the check. I 'm sure we were the last ones to leave church that morning, but no one even mentioned money. I was really disappointed. It is embarrassing now to think how ungrateful I was for all that people had done. I'm ashamed to think how hurt I felt when no one gave any money at all. I had my eyes on people. I was looking at the ground where I had been sowing seeds for years and I was very disappointed not to see an immediate harvest springing up for me to reap. I was even beginning to feel that God had not really taken care of all our needs.

Before the next Sunday meeting we received a letter in the mail from Sarah's mother. Her mother worked in the payroll division for the Dothan Police Department. In the letter was a check to us from the policemen where she worked. Even though we did not personally know any of those men and women, they had passed the hat and taken up a collection to help us when they heard about our dilemma. We were deeply touched and humbled by their outpouring of goodwill.

We learned a very important lesson. We are to sow abundantly as the Lord allows us to prosper and we are to believe that when we have a need we will reap an abundant supply. However, we are to always sow as unto the Lord. He is the Lord of the harvest. We are to keep our eyes on Him and not on the ground. As we fix our eyes on Jesus, He will instruct whomever he desires to meet our need. This has been such a valuable lesson for us to learn. As we keep our eyes on Jesus to meet our need, we are liberated to give freely and expect nothing in return. We don't get angry with those we think should and ought to meet our need in time of trouble.

Principle 19:

Everybody is afraid of something.

Let me repeat that: everybody is afraid of something. The sooner we all figure out what we are most afraid of, work down to what we are least afraid of and then gain the victory over those fears, the happier all of mankind will be.

The first consequence of sin was fear.

Genesis 3:7-10, "Then the eyes of both of them were opened, and they knew that they were naked; and they sowed fig leaves together and made themselves loin coverings.

8 And they heard the sound of the Lord God walking in the garden in the cool of the day, and the man and his wife hid themselves from the presence of the Lord God among the trees of the garden.

9 Then the Lord God called to the man, and said to him, 'Where are you?'

10 And he said, 'I heard the sound of Thee in the garden, and I was afraid because I was naked; so I hid myself.'"

Sin caused man to fear. Because man was afraid, he made a wrong decision based on his fear. Adam told God, "...I was afraid...so I hid myself." From Adam and Eve to all generations since, man has

201

inherited that sinful nature which is always prone to fear. Almost all decisions based on fear, instead of faith, are apt to be the wrong decision. The last part of Romans 14:23 proclaims boldly that "...whatever is not of faith is sin."

In first John, John makes "fear" the opposite of "love." John tells believers:

"There is no fear in love; but perfect love casts out fear, because fear involves punishment, and the one who fears is not perfected in love" 1 John 4:18.

Perfect love (*agape*) casts out fear. Fear is self-centeredness. Fear focuses only on me, what is going to happen to me. Love focuses on others. Therefore, if God's perfect love, His *agape* (same as I Corinthians 13:4-8), is present fear, or self-centeredness, cannot remain. One will drive out the other. Since God's love is greater than anything else, and is eternal, it will always drive out fear.

When I teach my Public Speaking class about ways to overcome stage fright, I always tell my students that one way to overcome the fear of speaking in front of a live audience is to concentrate on communicating with the audience. Fear is concentrating on yourself. It is thinking, "Oh, they don't like me," or, "I'm terrible," or, "I think I'm gonna die." Rather, think about your audience. Ask yourself, "Do they understand what I just said," or, "Do I need to use simple words or even go to a higher level?" If you genuinely care about your audience and the message you are communicating, you will not think about yourself and yield to the fear. I believe it is a Biblical principle.

We have many Biblical examples of great men who felt fear and made wrong decisions based on that fear. After Adam, Abraham is one of our first great men who had a weakness in this area. On two different occasions Abraham feared for his life and told a half truth about his wife, Sarah. In Genesis 12:10-20 Abraham goes to Egypt but fears that he will be killed so that the Egyptians can have his beautiful wife. He tells Sarah to lie by saying she is his sister. Pharaoh takes her into his household and treats Abraham very nicely because of his beautiful sister. God rescues Sarah by sending plagues on Pharaoh's household until he realizes what Abraham has done.

Years later, Abraham takes his family to Gerar (Genesis 20:1-18) and once again fears he will be killed because of his beautiful wife. King Abimelech takes Sarah into his household until God appears to him in a dream and says, "Behold, you are a dead man, because of the woman whom you have taken; for she is a man's wife" (v. 3). Again, God rescues Sarah, the obedient wife.

Both these events happened before Isaac was born (Genesis 21:1-3). Isaac did not personally witness his father do these things. Yet years later, when he has a wife, Rebekah, he repeats the sin of his father. Isaac, too, goes to Gerar due to a famine (Genesis 26:6-11). He too fears for his life because of his beautiful wife and lies that she is his sister.

King Abimelech looked out a window one day and saw Isaac "fondling" (RSV) Rebekah and confronts Isaac. Abimelech is so upset he warns all the people that "Whoever touches this man or his wife shall be put to death." (v. 11). We see a pattern of sin repeated in the life of the son.

By the third generation, the grandson is even named "deceiver." The deceiver, Jacob, also continues to lie as he pretends to be his elder brother, Esau. Acting in fear and then lying, which often work together, seem to run in the family.

Jacob ran away from Esau fearing for his life [Genesis 27:45]. Years later he is returning to his father and brother but still has this dreadful fear that his brother will kill him [Genesis 32]. In desperation Jacob cries out to God for deliverance, reminding God of the promises He had made when he first fled from Esau. It is God's grace and mercy that the angel wrestled with Jacob until daybreak. Finally when the angel dislocates Jacob's hip, Jacob can no longer depend on himself and his deceiving, lying ways. He is changed when he realizes he must put his faith in God. Instead of walking in fear, he must "limp in faith." We all "limp in faith" when we begin! We all limp in faith before we walk in faith, and walk in faith before we learn to live by faith.

Moses was another great leader who suffered from anxiety attacks. Moses was afraid to go back to Egypt even with God speaking to him from a burning bush. After all, he had run away from Egypt because he feared for his life. Forty years in the desert had not dimmed that fear. Notice the conversation he has with God.

Exodus 3:10-12, "Therefore, come now, and I will send you to Pharaoh, so that you may bring My people, the sons of Israel, out of Egypt.

11 But Moses said to God, 'Who am I, that I should go to Pharaoh, and that I should bring the sons of Israel out of Egypt? '

12 And He said, 'Certainly I will be with you, and this shall be the sign to you that it is I who have sent you: when you have brought the people out of Egypt, you shall worship God at this mountain.'"

Exodus 4:1-3, Then Moses answered and said, "What if they will not believe me, or listen to what I say? For they may say, 'The Lord has not appeared to you.'"

2 And the Lord said to him, 'What is that in your hand?' And he said, 'A staff.'

3 Then He said, 'Throw it on the ground.' So he threw it on the ground, and it became a serpent; and Moses fled from it."

Exodus 4:10-15, "Then Moses said to the Lord, 'Please, Lord, I have never been eloquent, neither recently nor in time past, nor since Thou hast spoken to Thy servant; for I am slow of speech and slow of tongue.'

11 And the Lord said to him, "Who has made man's mouth? Or who makes him dumb or deaf, or seeing or blind? Is it not I, the Lord?

12 Now then go, and I, even I, will be with your mouth, and teach you what you are to say.

13 But he said, 'Please, Lord, now send the message by whomever Thou wilt.'

14 Then the anger of the Lord burned against Moses, and He said, 'Is there not your brother Aaron the Levite? I know that he speaks fluently. And moreover, behold, he is coming out to meet you; when he sees you, he will be glad in his heart.

15 And you are to speak to him and put the words in his mouth; and I, even I, will be with your mouth and his mouth, and I will teach you what you are to do. "

Moses was so afraid he pushed God until "the anger of the Lord burned against him." It took quite a bit of convincing and the assurance that his older brother, Aaron, would go with him to get Moses to overcome his fear. God did what was necessary to help Moses gain the victory so that he could fulfill God's destiny for his life.

Years later the mighty prophet of fire, Elijah, was so overcome with horror at the thoughts of what Queen Jezebel might do to him that he ran for his life and begged God to take him home.

1 Kings 19:1-4, "Now Ahab told Jezebel all that Elijah had done, and how he had killed all the prophets with the sword.
2 Then Jezebel sent a messenger to Elijah, saying, 'So may the gods do to me and even more, if I do not make your life as the life of one of them by tomorrow about this time. '
3 And he was afraid and arose and ran for his life and came to Beersheba, which belongs to Judah, and left his servant there.
4 But he himself went a day's journey into the wilderness, and came and sat down under a juniper tree; and he requested for himself that he might die, and said, 'It is enough; now, O Lord, take my life, for I am not better than my fathers'"

God did not smite His fearful prophet but fed him by angels and gently spoke to him through a small, still voice. In the end He gave him a new servant, Elisha, to stand with him to finish his God ordained task.

Many generations later, Jeremiah following in the prophetic footsteps of Elijah also had to overcome his fears to be God's voice to His people.

**Jeremiah 1:4-8 (KJV), "Then the word of the LORD came unto me, saying,
5 Before I formed thee in the belly I knew thee; and before thou camest forth out of the womb I sanctified thee, and I ordained thee a prophet unto the nations.
6 Then said I, Ah, Lord GOD! behold, I cannot speak: for I am a child."
7 But the LORD said unto me, Say not, I am a child: for thou shalt go to all that I shall send thee, and whatsoever I command thee thou shalt speak.
8 Be not afraid of their faces: for I am with thee to deliver thee, saith the LORD.**

In the New Testament, Peter is probably our most outstanding example of a bold, yet fearful disciple. Peter acted out of fear on several (if not many) occasions. Our Lord Jesus worked with Peter again and again to help him gain mastery over his fears. Finally Peter was able to be established in victory over his fears and could write confidently:

**1 Peter 5:8-11, "Be of sober spirit, be on the alert. Your adversary, the devil, prowls about like a roaring lion, seeking someone to devour.
9 But resist him, firm in your faith, knowing that the same experiences of suffering are being accomplished by your brethren who are in the world.
10 And after you have suffered for**

a little while, the God of all grace, who called you to His eternal glory in Christ, will Himself perfect, confirm, strengthen and establish you.
11 To Him be dominion forever and ever. Amen."

After so many bad decisions based on fear, Peter was convinced that God is a "God of all grace" and that He "will Himself perfect, confirm, strengthen and establish you" because He alone has all "dominion forever and ever." Like Peter, we all have to see that we are afraid of something. Like Peter we all have to learn to receive God's mercy so we can overcome. Like Jacob we have to learn to "limp in faith" before we can walk in faith and later live by faith.

Principle 20:

Everybody has expectations.

Whether spoken or unspoken, known or unknown, expectations reside deep within each person who makes a new friend, starts a new job, gets married or comes to your church. There is probably no true middle ground, no absolute neutral point on any continuum in the human psyche. In every situation we enter, every new relationship we start, we bring with us some degree of expectation about the outcome of that encounter. Without any rational explanation we may experience excitement and fulfillment or disappointment and emptiness. When we cannot explain why, it is probably because of some unmet expectation(s) that we were not even aware we had.

Living Way Church was founded in Shizuoka city on May 12, 1988. Our church's membership is composed of new converts with virtually no Christian background and those who have come to us from other churches representing a great variety of cultural and religious experiences. I have been amazed that both groups still have expectations of what our church is supposed to be. Of course the most opinionated group by far is the group with previous church experience. Let me just give one of many examples.

In the Kings James Version of 1 Corinthians 14:40 it says, "Let all things be done decently and in order." This is a great verse as long as we allow God to define "decently" and "in order." Everyone has their own definition (and expectations) of what these words mean. If you come from a "high church" background, this means "...the Lord is in His holy temple. Let all the earth be silent before Him" (Habakkuk 2:20. There must be a "solemn assembly" in which everything follows a definite ritual, with no deviation. If you come from a charismatic group that met at the local "Kiddy Kollege" near the university (which is part of my background) "decently" and "in order" virtually means anything goes as long as we don't get too indecent. How do we determine what is decent and orderly in God's opinion? Jesus is the Head of the Body, His church, so what does He consider correct? Sometimes our definition seems to be His definition until something happens to make us question what we've laid down as "God's way."

In 1976 I was the faculty sponsor for an interdenominational Christian club at the local community college where I taught speech. That year a young minister took my public speaking class and we became friends. He came to our club room one day to talk to me about what had happened at the large Baptist church where he was serving as an assistant minister. The previous Sunday morning they had a large crowd as usual consisting of faithful saints and visitors. After the very first song, a man got up, walked to the front and stood at the communion table below the pastor's pulpit. Nobody knew what to do. One of the deacons quickly moved to the front and asked the man what he was doing. The man said, "I want to get saved."

The deacon said, "It's not time yet. Please sit down."

The man insisted, "I want to get saved now." He

didn't move.

The embarrassed deacon explained, "It's not time yet. Look at your program. We have to sing four more songs and take up an offering. Then the preacher gives his sermon and THEN you can come forward and get saved." After an awkward, mumbled conversation the man finally walked off to a side room with the deacon.

The young minister was shaken by this experience. He looked at me and said, "You know, I think something is wrong with our program when we can't allow a man to get saved when he's ready! We're Baptists for crying out loud!" I agreed with the young minister. However, the deacon was just trying to keep things in proper order and many probably applauded his efforts at doing the decent thing.

One Sunday morning in Japan we had a particularly expressive move of the Holy Spirit. An American who had only visited our church a few times came to me toward the end (I say toward the end because it was one of those meetings that I did not know how or when to end). He said, "Wow, I've never been to a church like this. You have all kinds of things happening all over the room. This is great!" Looking about the room we had some people peacefully lying on the floor as if they were sleeping. Others were lying on the floor weeping and/or shaking. In the back one lady had the "holy giggles." Elsewhere people were still kneeling and praying very reverently. Some were laying hands on others and praying in English or Japanese or Indonesian or only the Lord knows what other language. We sometimes have so many different native languages represented among our congregation I've given up on saying that person is speaking in tongues. I was standing in front alternately praying and looking around. I certainly was not directing this meeting. It had long before gone beyond anything I could control.

I was glad the American man had such a positive response. Someone else with a different background could have had a very different reaction. What we have to determine is who defines what is correct order? I still don't have a good definition except that "we [must] have as our ambition... to be pleasing to Him" (2 Corinthians 5:9).

Being in the presence of Jesus provokes a response. When Jesus walks in demons cry out; hearts are opened and sorrow or joy come forth; gifts start to function as faith arises for people to prophesy and speak in tongues; and all sorts of unexpected things happen. Because you really don't know what is inside people and you don't know what is going to come out. I believe Jesus had very noisy meetings. Jesus is the only man the Bible says received the spirit without measure. When the awesome fullness of the Holy Spirit came into a room with Jesus, people and demons had to respond. There was absolutely no middle ground. Nobody like Him had ever walked the face of the earth since the garden of Eden.

Almost twenty years ago, I was in a meeting in the small village of Rambaccum, Tamil Nadu in south India. We met in the local doctors house because it was the largest home available. Almost no one in the meeting had been a Christian for more than a year. All were converts from Hinduism. Ian

Brille, a missionary friend who lived in India, and I were sitting up front. Our interpreter and worship leader, Mohan, was leading the singing. The singing quickly escalated from praise to intense worship that got louder and stronger. The new believers were getting more and more lost in the presence of God as he "enthroned Himself on their praises." A group of unsaved Hindus stood along the back wall watching our every move.

The worship went on and on. Some were clapping their hands, singing and bouncing on their knees on the floor in an acrobatic way that I could not begin to emulate. I leaned over to Mohan and asked, "Can you calm them down?"

"No. I lost control of this meeting a long time ago," Mohan replied with a grin.

Right at my feet an elderly lady started writhing on the floor like a snake. Her tongue flickered in and out just like the dancing cobra's I'd seen in the market. My eyes got as big as the Hindus' standing against the back wall. Demons were manifesting in God's presence. Ian reached out and touched the woman. She fell on the floor like she was dead. At that instant the bare light bulb protruding from the kitchen wall exploded and fire shot out of the socket. The Hindus ran out of the doctor's house. The elderly lady sat up, brushed herself off and smiled. She was gloriously set free.

In the midst of this activity the worship never slowed down. They didn't skip a syllable. I didn't say anything else about calming everybody down. We worshipped until God had fulfilled His Expectations for that meeting. Then, and only then, was it time to stop singing and preach! Jesus is the only one who has the right to determine what is decent and in order. Therefore, Jesus' expectations are the only ones that really matter in the long run. We must seek to know what He expects and live up to those expectations.

Principle 21:

No one is truly neutral about anything.

I've been teaching communication and public speaking classes for the past thirty years. I still remember and teach what I learned in a course titled "The Psychology of Persuasion." Using a Likert type scale I show a range from minus ten to positive ten with zero in the center. I explain what needs to be done to overcome negative attitudes, minus ten being the most extreme, and what we can do to strengthen positive attitudes and to prevent against counter-persuasion the positive person may face from others. All of this material seems rather logical to most students and may even be old knowledge for them. They wake up when I say that even though we have a place marked zero on the scale there is no absolute neutral point.

What we call neutral is usually assumed to be a place where we have no feelings or opinions about the topic at hand. This may be close to the truth on some matters but even then everyone will have a slight leaning toward negative or positive based on what they think the topic is or, perhaps, based on the sound of the words. Of the three types of neutral attitudes I discuss, this one is called the "Ignorant Neutral." Basically this means you are hovering around the zero marker simply because you lack enough information to have an informed opinion. To move someone off this point you simply need to supply the missing information. As soon as you supply some information, preconceived ideas, past experiences and bits of knowledge about related subjects will join in to rapidly push the person toward the positive or the negative. In this day of information overload it is difficult to be in a truly zero position because of total ignorance on almost any subject.

The other two types of neutral attitudes represent anything but an absence of feelings or opinions. These two attitudes represent "Intense Neutral Attitudes" that are exact opposites. The first "Intense Neutral Attitude" is the "Approach-Approach Conflict." This is the person who "wants his cake and eat it too." This person has intense positive feelings toward two choices. He is in the middle simply because he cannot choose between two good things. For example, let's say Julie has two suitors, Frank and Charlie. Both propose marriage, but Julie can't make a decision. Frank is strong and athletic and great fun. Charlie is intelligent, a very interesting conversationalist and comes from a wealthy family. Julie likes them both, but in different ways. She's stuck in the middle simply because she cannot decide on which one is a better choice.

The other "Intense Neutral Attitude" is the "Avoidance-Avoidance Conflict." This is what we call "caught between a rock and a hard place." This person has equally intense negative feelings toward two options. He is in the middle because he cannot choose between what he perceives as two equally bad choices. Imagine that you are taking a linguistics class. The professor tells the class that your grade for the entire course will be based on one of two options. You may give a fifteen minute oral presentation

218

from memory before the class or you may write a ten page term paper on some current area of research in linguistics. You're stymied. You are terrified of public speaking and could never survive the stress of a fifteen minute presentation from memory. On the other hand, you don't know anything about linguistics. What you do know you don't like and you've never made a good grade on a term paper. You feel doomed. How can you choose between two equally bad choices?

Both intense neutral attitudes are very real and very difficult to overcome. Our attitudes and opinions are based on our beliefs and values. Therefore we must help the person determine which value/belief is more important. Then they can move in the direction that best represents that value.

For a Christian it may be a problem like my wife, Sarah, experienced. She was working part-time at a local health care facility. Before the upcoming inspection that would determine whether the facility continued to be licensed , the head of the facility dropped by her department. He informed her that her department was the key to keeping the facility operational. He then told her that prior to her working there her department had not followed proper procedures of cleanliness and testing. However, the records had been "doctored" to show that they had. He instructed her to verify the records when asked by the inspectors.

This presented an immediate conflict for my wife. She had two conflicting values. One, she believed that as a Christian worker she was to obey the authority over her and be the best possible worker. To her boss that meant lying about the records. Second, she believed that as a Christian she should always tell the truth, no matter what the consequences. Either choice represented negative consequences for her. If she told the truth, according to her boss, the facility would be closed down. Many fine people would lose their jobs and other equally fine people would not receive the health care they needed. On the other hand, if she lied she would have to live with the guilt of acting contrary to a belief that was very central to her convictions.

We considered her options and even the possibility of her taking a day of personal leave when the inspectors came. Sarah felt she needed to face the situation and not hide at home. She decided to go to work and tell the truth. We covered that decision with much prayer. In the end the inspectors came but never mentioned anything about the past reports but were only interested in current procedures (which had corrected the problem).

Not everyone is blessed with such a solution. I have known several people in Japan, India and Indonesia who were given a choice between becoming a Christian or remaining in their family. They were told, "You cannot be a Japanese and be a Christian" or, "You cannot be a Christian and be part of this family" or "You become a Christian and you'll not receive any of your inheritance." This is still the decision that many people face all over the world. They are forced to choose between identifying with Christ or identifying with their family, culture or nation. Some find themselves in "intense neutral," unable to move in either direction.

This is not a new phenomena. This is why Jesus said, "He who is not with Me is against Me; and he who does not gather with Me, scatters" (Luke 11:23). There is no zero on Jesus' scale, only positive or negative. Our goal is to persuade as many as possible to abandon their negative position, no matter how neutral it may seem, and choose Jesus. I like the way Moses explained it to the children of Israel just before he died.

**Deuteronomy 30:19-20a, "I call heaven and earth to witness against you today, that I have set before you life and death, the blessing and the curse. So choose life in order that you may live, you and your descendants,
20 by loving the Lord your God, by obeying His voice, and by holding fast to Him; for this is your life and the length of your days... "**

There can be no neutral position about the most important decision in anyone's life. Encourage people to choose life and that Jesus is the only way to life!

Principle 22:

Some will put their own survival aboveall other principles they profess to believe.

In Proverbs there is a troubling verse regarding the faithlessness of men.

Proverbs 20:6 (KJV), "Most men will proclaim every one his own goodness: but a faithful man who can find?"

(NASV) "Many a man proclaims his own loyalty, But who can find a trustworthy man?"

We wish this verse were not true but we know that it is. Faithful, trustworthy friends are rare, and thus, very valuable. I believe Jesus was warning us about our own tendencies toward being disloyal when he told his disciples that they must be willing to lose their lives in order to save them.

**Matthew 16:24-26, "Then Jesus said to His disciples, If anyone wishes to come after Me, let him deny himself, and take up his cross, and follow Me.
25 For whoever wishes to save his life shall lose it; but whoever loses his life for My sake shall find it.
26 For what will a man be profited, if he gains the whole world, and forfeits his soul? Or what will a man give in**

223

exchange for his soul?"

Paul voices his agreement to Christ's words in his last letter to Timothy.

2 Timothy 2:11-13, "It is a trustworthy statement: For if we died with Him, we shall also live with Him;
12 If we endure, we shall also reign with Him; If we deny Him, He also will deny us;
13 If we are faithless, He remains faithful; for He cannot deny Himself."

This idea of denying oneself and laying down your life willingly for others goes against our basic instinct of self-preservation. Self-preservation goes far beyond the drive to stay alive. It includes preserving one's mental and emotional stability as well. Too often when we feel threatened in any way, we abandon the principles we have so nobly espoused before others.

Our last few years in America before coming to Japan were some of the most difficult we had experienced. God was preparing us for greater challenges and the training was stretching us to the breaking point. My wife had particularly been stretched when several former friends had turned against her over trivial matters.

For years she had been close to Clarisa only to have her, not only reject their friendship, but also go out of her way to tear down Sarah's relationships with others. Clarisa had a way of expressing herself that produced the illusion of humility and spirituality. Her distortions and insinuations took their toll on Sarah and her friends. Gradually though, most of Sarah's friends discerned what was happening and stood by her.

As the truth became more apparent to most people in the church, Sarah could not understand why her dear friend, Amy, had separated herself from the conflict. Sarah had stood with Amy through many trying times as she had struggled with her husband and children. Although Amy remained congenial, she would not take a stand with Sarah about the truth. She seemed to be playing both sides of the fence.

Before we left for the mission field Amy told Sarah that she knew Clarisa was wrong and that she had hurt Sarah. Even though Amy knew the truth she would not defend Sarah. She explained it very simply to my wife when she said, "Sarah, you're leaving and I have to live here. So I'm not going to upset Clarisa."

Although this was a painful lesson, my wife is a very forgiving person. She understood that Amy was very weak emotionally and could not stand the thought of being Clarisa's next victim. When Amy's emotional survival was threatened, she abandoned her principles and yielded to her self-preservation instinct.

Over the years I have observed that a man or a woman married to an extremely contentious and difficult person will do almost anything to keep peace at home. They will not take a stand for what is right if they are going to pay for it again and again with a difficult spouse.

Paul encourages us that, "If possible, so far as it depends on you, be at peace with all men" (Romans 12:18). The writer of Hebrews tells us to "Pursue peace with all men…" (Hebrews 12:14). But we are never told to chose "peace" at the expense of "truth." Any peace gained by compromising the Word of God or adjusting the facts will only be a temporary "absence of war."

When I talk to Japanese people about cultural differences between Japan and America I eventually discuss the ranking of values. Historically, Americans placed a higher value on "truth" and "honesty" than on "harmony." In Japan though, "harmony" is considered a greater value than "truth" or "honesty." If telling the truth is going to trouble the waters of a relationship, then telling a lie is considered more virtuous than telling the truth and destroying harmony. It does seem rather trivial to tell someone that their new hairstyle is lovely when in actuality it is most unbecoming. However it is not trivial to tell someone that their actions are not wrong or sinful because they will be offended when their deeds are clearly in violation of the scriptures and will lead to eternal separation from God. In writing to Timothy Paul refers to the church as "…the pillar and support of the truth" (1 Timothy 3:15). We should always support the truth regardless of how people respond.

Principle 23:
There is always another side of the Story

Proverbs 18:17 (Amplified Bible), "He who states his case first seems right, until his rival comes and cross-examines him."

Proverbs 18:13, "He who gives an answer before he hears, It is folly and shame to him."

From the beginning we see mankind trying to present only his side of the story in an effort to escape personal responsibility. When God challenged Adam by asking, "Have you eaten from the tree of which I commanded you not to eat?" Adam replied, "The woman whom Thou gavest to be with me, she gave me from the tree, and I ate." Notice that Adam blamed both "the woman" and "God" for his downfall. Adam said, "she, the woman, gave me from the tree," but "Thou gavest me the woman!" The woman, of course, blamed the serpent. The serpent had no one left to blame.

Adam's side of the story was that he was lead astray by his wife and God had a hand in it. Eve's side of the story was that she was deceived by the serpent. Of course, in this situation, God was the one asking the questions when he already knew the answers. We, on the other hand, do not always know

227

the answers to our questions. The problem is that we often do not even ask the questions. We hear one side of the story and proceed to act or react without hearing the other person's version. As the Proverbs warn, this often leads to folly and shame.

One Example of someone reacting without hearing the other side of the story is David. His son Absalom had seized the throne and David was fleeing for his life. He was met by Ziba who had been assigned to take care of Mephibosheth, former King Saul's handicapped son. David listened to Ziba without checking out Mephibosheth's version of the incident.

2 Samuel 16:1-4, "Now when David had passed a little beyond the summit, behold, Ziba the servant of Mephibosheth met him with a couple of saddled donkeys, and on them were two hundred loaves of bread, a hundred clusters of raisins, a hundred summer fruits, and a jug of wine.
2 And the king said to Ziba, 'Why do you have these?' And Ziba said, 'The donkeys are for the king's household to ride, and the bread and summer fruit for the young men to eat, and the wine, for whoever is faint in the wilderness to drink.'
3 Then the king said, 'And where is your master's son?' And Ziba said to the king, 'Behold, he is staying in Jerusalem, for he said, 'Today the house of Israel will restore the kingdom of my

father to me.'
4 So the king said to Ziba, 'Behold, all
that belongs to Mephibosheth is yours.'
And Ziba said, 'I prostrate myself; let
me find favor in your sight, O my lord,
the king!'"

When David finally hears from Mephibosheth, his
judgment does not seem equitable. He only restores
half of Mephibosheth's land and lets the deceiver,
Ziba, keep half.

2 Samuel 19:24-30, "Then Mephibosheth
the son of Saul came down to meet the
king; and he had neither cared for his feet,
nor trimmed his mustache, nor washed his
clothes, from the day the king departed
until the day he came home in peace.
25 And it was when he came from
Jerusalem to meet the king, that the
king said to him, 'Why did you not go
with me, Mephibosheth?'
26 So he answered, 'O my lord, the
king, my servant deceived me; for your
servant said, 'I will saddle a donkey for
myself that I may ride on it and go with
the king,' because your servant is lame.
27 Moreover, he has slandered your
servant to my lord the king; but my
lord the king is like the angel of God,
therefore do what is good in your
sight.

28 For all my father's household was nothing but dead men before my lord the king; yet you set your servant among those who ate at your own table. What right do I have yet that I should complain anymore to the king?'
29 So the king said to him, 'Why do you still speak of your affairs? I have decided, You and Ziba shall divide the land.'
30 And Mephibosheth said to the king, 'Let him even take it all, since my lord the king has come safely to his own house.'"

No one knows why David only restored half of Mephibosheth's land. Perhaps he was really suspicious of Mephibosheth or perhaps he was embarrassed and wanted to "save face." Whatever motivated David's final decision, he should have listened to both sides of the story before reapportioning lands and inheritance.

Principle 24:

People want to be in control.

"Daddy Blount, when are you coming to Japan?" I asked my step-father on one of my trips back to Alabama.

"As soon as they build a bridge I'll be there," he quipped.

Adding a knowledgeable commentary my mother said, "If they would let him fly the plane, he'd come. He's got to be in control."

My father had his reasons for not flying to Japan or anywhere. I remember him telling me the stories when I was young. When he was in the Army during World War II, the Air Force was offering free flights to some of the earth bound infantry. My father got in line with many others eagerly anticipating their first flight. The plane reached its capacity just before he boarded. He'd have to wait for the next flight. As he and the others stood in awe they watched the twin-engine plane take off with their friends. Moments later they watched helplessly as the plane crashed, killing all on board. He decided he was not meant to fly in airplanes.

Years later, Daddy Blount was working as a federal fireman at Fort Benning in Columbus, Georgia. He and a friend were sitting on the back porch of the fire station when two helicopters flew overhead on a training mission. My father commented to his friend, "Now I think I might be willing to fly in one of those things."

As they watched the helicopters fly into the forest, the two firemen saw the helicopters disappear below the tree line. A rising column of black smoke followed the sound of an explosion. Just minutes later, the firemen were pulling the charred remains out of the twisted metal and melted plastic of the whirlybirds. That was the final confirmation to my father that God did not want him to fly, in anything.

I never argued with Daddy Blount about his decision. Those two events had forever seared themselves on the emotional fabric of his being. But, on the other hand, I don't think my mother was wrong either. Daddy Blount was a hard working, self-made man who had grown up during the depression. His father had gone blind when Daddy Blount was eleven years old and he had dropped out of school to take over the responsibilities of the farm. His father died shortly thereafter leaving him the major responsibility of providing for the family. Three years later the Great Depression made his responsibilities that much more difficult.

Through hard work and personal sacrifice Daddy Blount survived and prospered. He knew he could not depend on others to take care of him so he learned to take charge and get the job done. God blessed his perseverance and hard work. One result of all this hardship and success was the feeling that he should be in control of his own life. He could not depend on the government or family or any other person to ensure his survival. He didn't like other people to drive when he took a trip by car and he certainly wasn't going to sit forty rows back and let another man, especially a stranger, take him thirty thousand feet into the air!

Daddy Blount's not that unusual though. Most people like to either be in control or, at least, have the feeling that they are somewhat in control. Isn't this one reason that King Saul kept disobeying God's commands as delivered by Samuel. In I Samuel 13 (see Principle 15), Saul felt he was losing control of the situation as he waited seven days for Samuel to come sacrifice to the Lord. An overwhelmingly larger enemy arrayed themselves against Israel. Saul's soldiers were deserting and hiding themselves in caves and cellars and pits. Some even fled to other nearby countries. The King felt helpless, out of control. So he took charge. He ordered, "Bring to me the burnt offering and the peace offerings." And he offered the burnt offering"(v. 9). It made perfectly good sense to Saul. Samuel rebuked him as acting foolish in his disobedience.

Saul's final condemning sin was the result of his taking control, no matter what act of disobedience it required. Samuel had died. God wouldn't speak to him any more and the Philistines had returned seeking revenge.

**1 Samuel 28:5-7, "When Saul saw the camp of the Philistines, he was afraid and his heart trembled greatly.
6 When Saul inquired of the Lord, the Lord did not answer him, either by dreams or by Urim or by prophets.
7 Then Saul said to his servants, 'Seek**

**for me a woman who is a medium, that
I may go to her and inquire of her.'
And his servants said to him, 'Behold,
there is a woman who is a medium at
En-dor.'"**

Although Saul knew the punishment for consulting
a medium was death, he had to take control of his
predicament. He must know what to do. Instead of
repenting and returning to the Lord (the Lord's way),
he would have it his own way. In so doing, he sealed
his doom. The end of the story recorded in I Chronicles
states clearly why Saul died.

**1 Chronicles 10:13-14, "So Saul died
for his trespass which he committed
against the Lord, because of the word
of the Lord which he did not keep;
and also because he asked counsel of a
medium, making inquiry of it,
14 and did not inquire of the Lord.
Therefore He killed him, and turned the
kingdom to David the son of Jesse."**

It's not just kings and fathers who grew up during
the Great Depression who want to be in control. All
of us have this desire to be the master of our destiny.
If that is too abstract for some, then we just want to
have control over certain areas of our lives. Anyone
serving in a leadership capacity, whether at work or
in church, wants at least some degree of control over
the events that directly affect them. This has become
more and more real to me as we have sought to give

the Holy Spirit greater freedom among us in our meetings. As the pastor, part of me is saying, "Come Holy Spirit. Reveal more of Jesus among us. Have your own way. Do whatever you want." Another part of me is saying, "But, let me know what you are going to do before you do it and please, don't do anything that will embarrass me." Those two requests are usually in conflict. Let me explain an event in the life of our church that brought this home to me in a very tangible way.

After the service one Sunday about half the church people were still fellowshipping with one another when Pepito and his wife, Aki, approached my wife and I. The look on their faces indicated something serious. Pepito, a South Asian piano player who worked in a local night club, was usually very cheerful and light hearted, but not today. He explained that Aki, his Japanese wife from Kyushu, had received an ominous report from her gynecologist. Her doctor was almost certain she had a malignant tumor in her womb. She was to return for further tests on Tuesday to confirm the doctor's diagnosis. The doctor's prognosis was not good. They were very concerned not only for Aki but for their two small children.

I looked around the room to see who could join us for prayer. I called Junko, a young woman who had recently been filled with the Holy Spirit and was always excited to pray, to agree with us for Aki's healing. We all felt the gravity of the situation so much that we did not want to rush into verbalizing our concerns. As we waited on the Holy Spirit to guide us, Junko began moaning in her naturally high-pitched voice. The longer we waited the more intense the groaning grew. Before we knew what was happening, Junko's high-pitched wailing had reached an intensity that actually hurt my ears.

It is amazing how many thoughts and feelings can career through your brain in a few seconds. One of my first thoughts was, "I hope Winston and Hillary are gone." They had particularly been against the recent unusual manifestations of the Holy Spirit among us. A quick survey of the room relieved me of that worry. They had gone home early.

Another thought was "the neighbors. We better close the windows and doors!" Although several were open, I was not in a position to slip away and close anything. Besides, as I looked around the room I was surprised that no one seemed to be disturbed by Junko's shrill moaning. I was especially surprised that neither Pepito nor Aki were upset. Actually the more intense Junko became the more peaceful Aki looked. I seemed to be the most alarmed person in the room.

I finally turned to my wife and asked, "Is this the Holy Spirit or a demon or what?" My wife is usually very discerning but in this case she shook her head and said, "I don't know." Before I could discern the source of these emanations, they stopped. Everyone seemed serene, except me.

Since I was the pastor, I closed with a prayer for Aki's healing and encouragement. I was eager to leave lest someone ask me to explain what had just happened. After all, I was supposed to be the one in authority, yet I had no explanation for what we had just experienced. I had definitely been forced beyond my comfort zone. What kept me from making a hasty judgment based on my emotions, was the way all this had ministered to the person with the need. Aki seemed much better after having been shrieked at for what seemed like an eternity. One verse kept ringing through my head, "Therefore judge nothing before the time, until the Lord come, who both will bring to light the hidden things of darkness, and will make manifest the counsels of the hearts: and then shall every man have praise of God" (I Corinthians 4:5 KJV). So I decided to wait and pray until the test results on Tuesday.

Pepito called Tuesday afternoon before I returned home from work. My wife said he was crying so hard that she almost couldn't understand what he was trying to communicate. Finally she understood. The doctors checked Aki's womb again and again. They were very confused. The tumor that had been so visible only a week before was completely gone. They finally had to tell her and send her home. There was no trace of what they were certain was a cancerous growth.

Aki was very excited and relieved that she would not have to endure months of chemotherapy. Pepito was elated that he had his wife back and that he would not be left to care for two small children. The church rejoiced with those who were rejoicing and I learned a very valuable lesson about what is most important.

What was more important, that I be in control or that a woman get healed? Was it more important for me to remain comfortable or for a husband to get his wife back? Was it more important for me to have an answer for everything that happens or that two small children be raised by both their parents, instead of just one? My being uncomfortable meant nothing in comparison to what God had done in this family. Allowing the Holy Spirit to be in control means we are not in control. If we want to do what Jesus did, then we have to let Him have His unrestricted way among us.

As a postscript, let me add two bits of information. One, to this day, no one has complained about the shrieking nor have they asked me to explain it. And, two, it is now six years later and Aki is still completely healed!

Principle 25:

There is none good, no not one!

Mark 10:18 (KJV), "And Jesus said unto him, Why callest thou me good? there is none good but one, that is, God."

The pianist started her progression from lively praise music to a more worshipful one as the congregation made the transition into adoration. I did not enter into adoration with them. Instead, I entered the painful memories of rejection. This happened week after week. As everyone around me seemed to enter the peace and joy of His presence, I entered the world of the emotionally wounded. Every time we slowed the pace and the clapping stopped and my thoughts were freed from reading the overhead transparencies, the unfairness of betrayal and injustice crowded into my thoughts. Where there should have been feelings of love and worship there was only an aching emptiness. The emotions were so real they rushed unbidden into my consciousness.

My wife and I had poured our time and energy and love into helping a group of Indonesians feel accepted and welcomed in our predominantly Japanese congregation. Traditionally most Japanese look down on other Asians. This attitude comes right into the church with all the other imperfections redeemed, but imperfect, believers bring. For about three years we had encouraged the Japanese to accept the Indonesians as equal in Christ. We had exhorted the Indonesians to faithfully persevere even when

239

they felt rejection. We stressed to both groups that each had something unique to contribute to the body of Christ that met in Shizuoka. Finally, we felt we were blending into a body of believers that looked past race and nationality.

Then my wife and I realized that the Indonesians we had helped in so many ways had been in the process of forming their own, separate church. When we confronted them, they reluctantly confirmed that this had been their plan almost from the beginning. We felt used and betrayed. My wife's great love for them had helped her overcome her feelings much quicker than I. I couldn't overcome the injustice of it all. I had really believed we all shared the same vision of having a church where people from every race, nation and tongue could gather as one. I felt we were almost achieving our vision. We had finally overcome the racial barriers among the Japanese. Now the people we had worked with, and for, had decided to separate from us. I was hurt and angry. It seemed that every time I sat peacefully before the Lord, either in worship or prayer, I would be overcome with my hurts.

This Sunday morning was no exception until the Holy Spirit interrupted my emotional upheaval. Just as unsolicited as the negative thoughts had come, the Holy Spirit spoke the words of Jesus to my heart. "There is none good but one, that is, God." Jesus was quoting from the Psalms.

Psalms 53:1-3, "The fool has said in his heart, 'There is no God,' They

are corrupt, and have committed abominable injustice; There is no one who does good.

2 God has looked down from heaven upon the sons of men, To see if there is anyone who understands, Who seeks after God.

3 Every one of them has turned aside; together they have become corrupt; There is no one who does good, not even one."

The words of the scriptures brought immediate conviction to my own heart. I was hurt and angry for what others had done and yet I was really no better than they. I am just as much a sinner as any one of those I was accusing. Paul wrote:

Romans 3:9-12, 23 "What then? Are we better than they? Not at all; for we have already charged that both Jews and Greeks are all under sin;

10 as it is written, 'There is none righteous, not even one;

11 There is none who understands, There is none who seeks for God;

12 All have turned aside, together they have become useless; There is none who does good, There is not even one.'

23 for all have sinned and fall short of the glory of God."

As the church worshiped, my own sins and past failures flashed through my mind. Seeing myself so clearly, the feelings of rejection and betrayal that had weighed so heavily on me just a few moments ago seemed as light and thin as the morning mist. Since I am in the same condition as those who hurt me, I must not judge them so harshly. I must forgive because I want to be forgiven. I must show mercy because I want to receive mercy. Yes, they hurt me but I have also hurt others.

I have always struggled with two of Jesus' statements that seem to be opposites. Jesus said, "Do not judge lest you be judged" (Matthew 7:1). But, he also said, "Do not judge according to appearance, but judge with righteous judgment" (John 7:24). It appears that we are told not to judge and yet we are also told that we must judge.

The passage in Matthew 7 instructs us to judge ourselves before we judge others. If I accurately judge myself, then I will see who I am in relation to God and to others. I am a sinner saved by grace just like everyone else. If I remove the log in my own eye before I point out the splinter in my brother's eye, then I will be far more compassionate and merciful in dealing with him. Only if I judge myself first and accurately can I judge righteously. I must always remember that I can stand before God only because of the righteousness of Christ.

Paul writes that our goal is that I "may be found in Him, not having a righteousness of my own derived from the Law, but that which is through faith in Christ, the righteousness which comes from God on the basis of faith," (Philippians 3:9). It was God that "made Him who knew no sin to be sin on our behalf, that we might become the righteousness of God in Him" (2 Corinthians 5:21).

We will be hurt and disappointed by people just as we ourselves will hurt and disappoint others. We must always remember that "there is none good, not even one" and that includes ME.

Principle 26:

What people don't say may be more important than what they do.

Read carefully John's account of the woman caught in adultery. Pay attention not only to what her accusers "say" but also to what they "do not say."

John 8:2-11, "And early in the morning He came again into the temple, and all the people were coming to Him; and He sat down and began to teach them.
3 And the scribes and the Pharisees brought a woman caught in adultery, and having set her in the midst,
4 they said to Him, 'Teacher, this woman has been caught in adultery, in the very act.
5 Now in the Law Moses commanded us to stone such women; what then do You say?'
6 And they were saying this, testing Him, in order that they might have grounds for accusing Him. But Jesus stooped down, and with His finger wrote on the ground.
7 But when they persisted in asking Him, He straightened up, and said to them, He who is without sin among you, let him be the first to throw a stone at her.

8 And again He stooped down, and wrote on the ground.

9 And when they heard it, they began to go out one by one, beginning with the older ones, and He was left alone, and the woman, where she was, in the midst.

10 And straightening up, Jesus said to her, Woman, where are they? Did no one condemn you?

11 And she said, 'No one, Lord.' And Jesus said, Neither do I condemn you; go your way. From now on sin no more."

The scribes and Pharisees quickly and accurately point out that (1) she was caught in the very act of adultery and (2) that the Law of Moses commands to stone such women. Unless something was different in Bible times than it is today, it takes two people to commit adultery. Therefore, if the woman was caught in "the very act of adultery" then that means they also caught a man in "the very act of adultery"! Where was the man? There is no mention of him.

Look carefully at the scriptures the scribes and Pharisees were quoting:

Leviticus 20:10-11, "If there is a man who commits adultery with another man's wife, one who commits adultery with his friend's wife, <u>the adulterer and the adulteress shall surely be put to death.</u>

11 If there is a man who lies with his father's wife, he has uncovered his

father's nakedness; <u>both of them shall surely be put to death</u>, their blood guiltiness is upon them."

[Underline added by author.]

The scribes and Pharisees only quoted that the woman, the adulteress shall surely be put to death, yet both verses clearly say that both the man and the woman shall be put to death. They conveniently left out the part about the man to serve their own purposes.

When I first came to Japan, I listened to a set of tapes on prayer by a well-known American pastor. While the majority of the teaching was excellent, one section caused me to stumble into condemnation. The pastor told how he got up every morning and prayed from 4:30 to 6:30. He taught that in order to pray you had to become more disciplined. He mentioned that he went to bed every night at 8:30 or 9:00 and said that if you would make a commitment to get up at 4:30 every morning then you would have no difficulty going to bed at 8:30 in the evening. He summed up this portion of his teaching by saying, "Any pastor who does not spend two hours a day in prayer is not worthy to stand in the pulpit." I was soundly convicted of my prayerlessness and felt totally hopeless of ever being worthy of standing before a congregation again.

I also marveled that the pastor of a large church could go to bed every night by 8:30. He must have his church trained well for they dare not have a crisis after 9:00 PM. I had never been a part of a group that only had problems during traditional working hours! At that point in my life I had a wife and 5 small children, was pioneering a church in Japan and was teaching English in 5 or 6 different places just to pay the bills. Some of my classes didn't even finish until ten o'clock at night and one class I taught at a coffee shop started at 7:00 in the morning. I didn't see any way I could live up to the schedule of prayer I had just heard about.

A few months later we were tremendously blessed to have brother Francis Vernon stay with us for two weeks. I had the privilege of taking him from place to place and listening to him share his marvelous insights from the Word in many different churches in our area. After he had shared on prayer one evening, I told him about the tapes I had listened to and how badly I felt about my lack of discipline. Brother Vernon remarked, "Oh yes, I know that brother quite well. I've spoken in his church before. He is a fine man of God. By the way, did he happen to mention in his teaching that he takes a two hour nap every afternoon after lunch?"

"No, that wasn't part of his teaching," I replied. I was dumbfounded.

"Oh, yes. He very religiously locks his office door and has his secretary hold all calls until he's finished his nap," he explained. Then, he added, "I wouldn't be so condemned if I were you."

Those little missing details, that little extra information not mentioned, may mean a great deal. Always ask the Lord to reveal to you the missing information. What is hidden that you don't see or know? He promises he will reveal those things to us.

1 Corinthians 4:5, "...but wait until the Lord comes who will both bring to light the things hidden in the darkness and disclose the motives of men's hearts..."

Hebrews 4:13, "And there is no creature hidden from His sight, but all things are open and laid bare to the eyes of Him with whom we have to do."

Job 28:11, "...what is hidden he brings out to the light.

Principle 27:

Taking up the offense of another only leads to your own downfall.

Proverbs 26:17, "Like one who takes a dog by the ears is he who passes by and meddles with strife not belonging to him."

Proverbs 3:30, "Do not contend with a man without cause, If he has done you no harm."

Proverbs 20:3, "Keeping away from strife is an honor for a man, But any fool will quarrel."

Shimei is an example of someone taking up the offense of another. As David is fleeing for his life, Shimei takes advantage of the occasion to curse the discouraged King.

2 Samuel 16:5-12, "When King David came to Bahurim, behold, there came out from there a man of the family of the house of Saul whose name was Shimei, the son of Gera; he came out cursing continually as he came.
6 And he threw stones at David and at all the servants of King David; and all the people and all the mighty men were

at his right hand and at his left.

7 And thus Shimei said when he cursed, "Get out, get out, you man of bloodshed, and worthless fellow!

8"The Lord has returned upon you all the bloodshed of the house of Saul, in whose place you have reigned; and the Lord has given the kingdom into the hand of your son Absalom. And behold, you are taken in your own evil, for you are a man of bloodshed!"

9 Then Abishai the son of Zeruiah said to the king, 'Why should this dead dog curse my lord the king? Let me go over now, and cut off his head.'

10 But the king said, 'What have I to do with you, O sons of Zeruiah? If he curses, and if the Lord has told him, 'Curse David,' then who shall say, 'Why have you done so?'

11 Then David said to Abishai and to all his servants, 'Behold, my son who came out from me seeks my life; how much more now this Benjamite? Let him alone and let him curse, for the Lord has told him.

12 Perhaps the Lord will look on my affliction and return good to me instead of his cursing this day.'"

Where did Shimei get all this bad info about David? He grew up in Saul's house. He may have never even met David. He had been poisoned by Saul. David's misfortune emboldened Shimei to take up the offense of Saul and attack David. David would not let his mighty men kill Shimei. However, it was this action that eventually lead to Shimei's execution.

When David was restored to his kingship, Shimei hastened to meet him and quickly repented for what he had done. Again, Abishai wanted to execute him but David refused. Twice David extended grace to Shimei.

However, the last thing David does before he dies is warn his son Solomon about Shimei.

1 Kings 2:8-9, "And behold, there is with you Shimei the son of Gera the Benjamite, of Bahurim; now it was he who cursed me with a violent curse on the day I went to Mahanaim. But when he came down to me at the Jordan, I swore to him by the Lord, saying, 'I will not put you to death with the sword.'
9 "Now therefore, do not let him go unpunished, for you are a wise man; and you will know what you ought to do to him, and you will bring his gray hair down to Sheol with blood."

Solomon, like his father, showed mercy to Shimei. He summoned him and gave him one final chance to walk uprightly.

253

1 Kings 2:36-37, "Now the king sent and called for Shimei and said to him, Build for yourself a house in Jerusalem and live there, and do not go out from there to any place.
37 For it will happen on the day you go out and cross over the brook Kidron, you will know for certain that you shall surely die; your blood shall be on your own head."

Shimei agreed to this sentence of never leaving Jerusalem and obeyed. For three years he remained in Jerusalem. Then two of his servants ran away to another city and Shimei went after them. As soon as Solomon was told that he had left Jerusalem he summoned Shimei and had his chief executioner, Benaiah, carry out the death sentence. Had Shimei never taken up the offense of Saul, he would not have come to such an ignoble end.

According to the Law of Moses, a witness is only valid if he is an "eye witness." One of the definitions of witness is "to see or know by reason of personal presence: have direct cognizance of: observe with one's own eyes or ears: be present as an observer at: experience by personal observation." *[Webster's Third New International Dictionary, computer]* Anyone who speaks about an event he did not see with his own eyes is either gossiping or bearing false witness.

The apostle John begins his first letter with this powerful evidentiary statement:

1 John 1:1-3, "What was from the beginning, what we have heard, what we have seen with our eyes, what we beheld and our hands handled, concerning the Word of Life--
2 and the life was manifested, and we have seen and bear witness and proclaim to you the eternal life, which was with the Father and was manifested to us--
3 what we have seen and heard we proclaim to you also, that you also may have fellowship with us; and indeed our fellowship is with the Father, and with His Son Jesus Christ."

Three times John says he is reporting what he has seen with his own eyes. Twice he says he is telling what he heard with his own ears. For good measure he mentions that he has also touched with his own hands the Word of Life about which he is writing. John wants to make it perfectly clear from the outset that what we are about to read is a valid testimony because he was an "eye witness."

Many times those who take up the offense of another were not eye witnesses. Therefore they were making judgments based on hearsay evidence. Hearsay evidence is not acceptable according to God's law.

Principle 28:

There will be unexpected and undeserved acts of kindness!

Just as there are unprovoked and unjust acts of cruelty and deceit, there will be unexpected and undeserved acts of kindness. Do not become so jaded and cynical that you are unable to receive genuine acts of altruism when they come.

If you are sowing acts of kindness, then you will reap acts of kindness. If you sow mercy and grace, then you will receive acts of mercy and grace. We must be careful not to become so suspicious of others that we constantly suspect and question their motives.

In 1986, I made my first trip to Malaysia. Due to flight connection delays, I had to spend one night in Singapore before flying out the next morning. On the flight from Tokyo to Singapore, the Chinese passenger next to me started asking questions about my trip. He was a businessman returning home from a business trip. When he learned I did not know anyone in Singapore and that I had not made any reservations at a hotel, he said he would take care of me. I said, "Oh, don't worry about me, I'll just find the nearest Y.M.C.A."

"Oh, no. You don't need to stay there," he insisted.

When we landed I followed him to a nearby taxi. He took me to a very nice, expensive looking, new hotel. I was uneasy about how much this was going to cost. At the front desk he told the clerk, "This man is a friend of mine. Give him my company discount on his room and take good care of him." As he dashed off for home I quickly thanked him.

My room was incredible. It had everything I could want and, I learned later, with my company discount it cost about the same as I would have paid at the Y.M.C.A. This unexpected and undeserved act of kindness was a special blessing to me before I entered the jungles of Borneo to spend two weeks with a tribe who had no running water, electricity or indoor toilets.

Although Jesus was about to be critized, we see that he was the willing recipient of Mary's anointing with costly perfume.

> **John 12:1-8, "Jesus, therefore, six days before the Passover, came to Bethany where Lazarus was, whom Jesus had raised from the dead.**
> **2 So they made Him a supper there, and Martha was serving; but Lazarus was one of those reclining at the table with Him.**
> **3 Mary therefore took a pound of very costly perfume of pure spikenard, and anointed the feet of Jesus, and wiped His feet with her hair; and the house was filled with the fragrance of the perfume.**
> **4 But Judas Iscariot, one of His disciples, who was intending to betray Him, said,**
> **5 'Why was this perfume not sold for three hundred denarii, and given to**

poor people?'
**6 Now he said this, not because he was
concerned about the poor, but because
he was a thief, and as he had the
money-box, he used to pilfer what was
put into it.
7 Jesus therefore said, 'Let her alone, in
order that she may keep it for the day of
My burial.
8 For the poor you always have with
you, but you do not always have Me.'"**

Jesus did not prevent Mary from anointing Him
with very expensive perfume. Although there were
those who objected for seemingly good reasons,
Jesus received her spontaneous act of kindness.

I remember the anxiety I felt as I boarded the
Tamil Nadu Express in New Delhi to start my first
solo trip to south India. I had always had someone
travel with me to help with the language and local
customs. However, no one was free to travel with me
this time. Besides, I had made many trips to India
and was fairly secure in my ability to get around.
But once those doors closed and the train started
moving, I felt very uneasy.

Although it takes 24 to 36 hours to travel the
1,333 kilometers [829 miles], the Tamil Nadu
Express is the fastest train between New Delhi and
Madras [now renamed Chennai]. I usually traveled in
the air-conditioned car. I had my own place for sitting
and at night there was a place to lie down. There was
no privacy since the car was open except for a few
curtains that could be pulled. During the night the car

Ricky Thomas Gordon

became very cold so there were sheets, a pillow and wool blankets available from the porter.

After dinner the people around me began preparing to lie down for the evening. Then I realized I had not asked for my bedding. The next time the porter whisked through our car I followed him out into the unair-conditioned corridor between the cars and asked for my bedding. In very broken Indian English he said that he would get me some sheets and a pillow but he didn't have any more blankets. I mentioned that it gets very cold at night in that car and that I needed a blanket. He just said, "No blankets," and walked away.

A middle aged Indian fellow wearing a lungi was standing near the open half door of the train smoking a cigarette and looking at the passing scenery. He had overheard my conversation. He quickly snapped at the porter in Hindi. I didn't understand anything he said but I could tell by his tone of voice and facial expressions that he was giving orders to the porter. As the porter disappeared into the next car, the man turned to me and said, "He'll bring your sheets and blanket in a minute."

We talked for a few minutes as the man finished his cigarette. He was a buyer dealing in precious stones. He was traveling to south India to purchase uncut stones to take back to New Delhi. He gave me some valuable advice about how to buy stones in India and what to avoid so I didn't get cheated. In just a few minutes the porter came through the doors of the next car, handed me my pillow, sheets and wool blanket and disappeared again without a word. The stone buyer explained, "When the porter said there were no more wool blankets, what he really meant was there were no more wool blankets in this car. I knew he was just too lazy to walk to the next car to find you one if you didn't make him. So I scolded him for treating a foreigner in such a way and told him to go find you a blanket."

I was ignorant of the true situation and had done nothing to deserve this stranger's kindness, yet he took it upon himself to see that my needs were properly met. He was God's provision and blessing for me and I gladly received that warm blanket as a gift from Him.

I never saw the Indian stone buyer or the Chinese businessman again. I have never had the opportunity to return the acts of kindness they bestowed upon me. I have even wondered if they were angels sent to minister to me [although it is hard to imagine an angel wearing a lungi and smoking a cigarette]. I just know that I have been the beneficiary of unprovoked and undeserved acts of kindness in almost every country in the world where I have traveled. I have learned to receive these as gifts from God. Although I can never directly repay those who have helped me, I can be the one who acts on behalf of others who are in need of an undeserved and unexpected act of kindness.

Perhaps this is what Peter is explaining about Jesus when he said, "You know of Jesus of Nazareth, how God anointed Him with the Holy Spirit and with power, and how He went about doing good, and healing all who were oppressed by the devil; for God was with Him" (Acts 10:38). Jesus went about "doing good." While we are praying for the power to heal those oppressed by

Ricky Thomas Gordon

the devil, don't forget to go about "doing good."

Principle 29:

The favor of God far outweighs the evil of men & devils.

"And let the favor of the Lord our God be upon us; and do confirm for us the work of our hands; Yes, confirm the work of our hands" (Psalms 90:17).

"You sinned."

"Yes, I did," I had to admit to my wife. "I was anxious for something."

As soon as she said, "You sinned," the scripture, "be anxious for nothing" flashed through my mind. I knew I was not supposed to worry but I had lost several nights' sleep over my first tax audit. I would lie down at night thinking I would fall asleep immediately only to remember the first visit to the city tax office. The visit was even more frightening because the middle aged Japanese man was so nervous confronting a foreigner about his taxes. He had seemed so intense and strict during our first meeting that my fear of the final visit increased every time I pondered that encounter.

Now it was over and I could understand how much time and energy (and sleep) had been wasted over evils that never materialized. We, and many others, had asked the Lord for mercy and favor as the taxman poured over my missionary deductions and asked question after question about what I had done. My fears ran amuck as I imagined calling the states and asking for what little inheritance I had left to be wired immediately to pay

263

off taxes and penalties. All those fears were needless.
We had received mercy and favor far beyond my feeble
expectations.

What I had feared about the man, his intense and
strict demeanor, had actually worked in my favor.
Although he did not allow me to use several key
deductions that I had taken ever since becoming a
missionary in Japan, he found two major deductions
that I did not know existed and had never taken. In
the end I received more deductions than I lost. At
the end of auditing my previous year's returns, he
announced that the office had decided not to audit the
other two years they were allowed to review. Before
the interview ended he said that if I was audited
again, I could refer the reviewer to him to explain
our situation. God's favor is far greater than any evil
intent man can have.

We see this principle operating very clearly in
the life of Joseph. As years of envy and jealousy
peaked at the sight of Joseph in his multicolored tunic
approaching to investigate their behavior on behalf of
his doting father, the brothers undeniably intended evil
against their younger brother. Their murderous intent to
abandon Joseph in the pit gave way, not to compassion,
but to greed. At the age of seventeen [Genesis 37:2]
Joseph was sold into a life of slavery in a foreign land.

After thirteen years of hardship and disappointment,
Joseph stands before Pharaoh and is promoted to the
second highest position in Egypt [Gen. 41:46]. Nine
years later, at the age of 39, he reveals himself to his
terrified brothers [Gen. 45:11]. Twenty-two years after
their betrayal, Joseph comforts his brothers by explaining
God's purpose in all that had happened.

Genesis 45:5-9, "And now do not be grieved or angry with yourselves, because you sold me here; for <u>God sent me</u> before you to preserve life.

6 For the famine has been in the land these two years, and there are still five years in which there will be neither plowing nor harvesting.

7And <u>God sent me</u> before you to preserve for you a remnant in the earth, and to keep you alive by a great deliverance.

8 Now, therefore, <u>it was not you who sent me here, but God;</u> and He has made me a father to Pharaoh and lord of all his household and ruler over all the land of Egypt.

9 Hurry and go up to my father, and say to him, 'Thus says your son Joseph, God has made me lord of all Egypt; come down to me, do not delay.'"

[Underline added by author.]

Principle 30:

Everyone suffers from ADS (Addition Deficit Syndrome).

"I'm almost 52 years old and I still can't add." Is this the confession of an adult with ADS (Addition Deficit Syndrome)? No, this is what ran through my mind as the Holy Spirit gave me revelation regarding one source of rejection in my life.

I had been studying what I called "David's Prayer of Openness" to the Lord. It is based on the end of Psalms 139 in which David invites the Lord to,

Psalms 139:23-24, "Search me, O God, and know my heart; Try me and know my anxious thoughts;
24 And see if there be any hurtful way in me, And lead me in the everlasting way."

[Underline added by author.]

The phrase, "hurtful way," is of particular interest in these verses. "hurtful," otseb, can be defined as "a pain" or "sorrow." "Way," derek, can be translated as "way, road, distance, journey, manner;" or, as "a way, path in which one goes." "Hurtful way" therefore could be translated "way of pain; way of sorrow; or walking in the path of pain or sorrow."

There are two ways to take the meaning of this verse, both of which are very much interrelated. One interpretation is that David is asking God to see if there is anything in him that causes him to hurt others. Another interpretation would be to think of

267

David asking God to show him if he is walking in a path of pain or sorrow. It could be that David has had so much pain, rejection and sorrow in his life that he continually proceeds down a path of pain and sorrow. He has been wounded in his soul and continually responds out of that pain. He needs healing, as when he cries unto the Lord,

> **Psalms 51:10-12, "Create in me a clean heart, O God, And renew a steadfast spirit within me.**
> **11 Do not cast me away from Thy presence, And do not take Thy Holy Spirit from me.**
> **12 Restore to me the joy of Thy salvation, And sustain me with a willing spirit."**

These two interpretations work together. If I am wounded in my soul and/or spirit, that means I am probably walking in a path of pain or sorrow. As I continue in that way, I will respond to others out of my pain and therefore I will hurt them. Hurting people tend to hurt others in the same way they were hurt.

One of the saddest statistics in sociology is that those who were abused as children are much more likely to grow up to abuse their children. It is a vicious cycle of pain and abuse. Those who were abused are following a way of pain that was inflicted upon them. It is a rut that was cut into their very soul and even though they may hate it, they are continuing in that way of pain and sorrow and inflicting it on their own children.

David not only asks God to show him about a hurtful way but confirms that God can and does heal.

> **Psalms 23:3, "He restores my soul; He guides me in the paths of righteousness For His name's sake."**

I want to come back to David later but first let's talk about the source of this "way of pain and sorrow." I believe we were all born with a root of rejection.

> **Romans 5:12-19, "Therefore, just as through one man sin entered into the world, and death through sin, and so death spread to all men, because all sinned**
> **13 for until the Law sin was in the world; but sin is not imputed when there is no law.**
> **14 Nevertheless death reigned from Adam until Moses, even over those who had not sinned in the likeness of the offense of Adam, who is a type of Him who was to come.**
> **15 But the free gift is not like the transgression. For if by the transgression of the one the many died, much more did the grace of God and the gift by the grace of the one Man, Jesus Christ, abound to the many.**

16 And the gift is not like that which came through the one who sinned; for on the one hand the judgment arose from one transgression resulting in condemnation, but on the other hand the free gift arose from many transgressions resulting in justification.

17 For if by the transgression of the one, death reigned through the one, much more those who receive the abundance of grace and of the gift of righteousness will reign in life through the One, Jesus Christ.

18 So then as through one transgression there resulted condemnation to all men, even so through one act of righteousness there resulted justification of life to all men.

19 For as through the one man's disobedience the many were made sinners, even so through the obedience of the One the many will be made righteous."

Romans 3:23, "For all have sinned and fall short of the glory of God."

We were all born with a root of rejection that goes all the way back to Adam. Adam's sin resulted in his separation from God and his rejection. He could no longer live in the Garden of Eden. He could no longer walk and talk with God in total openness. We are born with that rejection in us. We are born with a sinful nature that God rejects.

Why did this happen? Satan had a very good revelation of God. Yet, he chose to rebel against God. Satan was rejected. He was cast out of heaven. He dwells in eternal rejection. He is already sentenced to the lake of fire and eternal separation from God.

Since he was rejected, part of his revenge was to get Adam and Eve rejected. Satan lives under an eternal sentence of condemnation and rejection. He wants to heap that rejection on mankind.

From the moment of your conception in the womb of your mother to the moment you die, Satan wants to do everything he can to make you feel rejected like him. If possible,

1. He will have your mother reject you before she can give you birth.
2. He will have you rejected at birth and then have your family heap rejection on you.
3. He will have others around you make you feel rejected and unacceptable.

That rejection will manifest itself in many ways in you:
1. anger which leads to hatred and violence
2. competition which seeks approval and acceptance
3. ridicule and sarcasm of others to make yourself appear better
4. strong drive for success, accomplishment to gain self-esteem-seeking approval
5. seeking to please men rather than God
6. closing your heart to others for fear of further rejection

7. withdrawing from close relationships, which you
   desperately need

In other words, because you feel rejected, you reject others. **"Do unto them before they can do unto you!"** I say again that, hurting people tend to hurt others in the same way they were hurt. This is just the opposite of what God wants us to do.

> **2 Corinthians 1:3-4, "Blessed be the God and Father of our Lord Jesus Christ, the Father of mercies and God of all comfort;**
> **4 who comforts us in all our affliction so that we may be able to comfort those who are in any affliction with the comfort with which we ourselves are comforted by God."**

Instead of hurting people with the same hurt I have been hurt with; instead of rejecting others with the same rejection with which I was rejected; I am to comfort others with the same comfort that God has comforted me! But before I can do this, I must have that root of rejection destroyed!

When you are born again, Jesus puts to death that original root of rejection. You are no longer rejected by God. You now have forgiveness of sins and can boldly enter into the presence of God.

Jesus, the good shepherd, wants to guide us in the paths of righteousness, in the everlasting way. He fully understands all that we have gone through and will ever face.

Hebrews 4:15, "For we do not have a high priest who cannot sympathize with our weaknesses, but One who has been tempted in all things as we are, yet without sin."

In Isaiah we clearly see that Jesus understands our rejection.

Isaiah 53:3-6, "He was despised and forsaken of men, A man of sorrows, and acquainted with grief; And like one from whom men hide their face, He was despised, and we did not esteem Him.
4 Surely our griefs He Himself bore, And our sorrows He carried; Yet we ourselves esteemed Him stricken, Smitten of God, and afflicted.
5 But He was pierced through for our transgressions, He was crushed for our iniquities; The chastening for our well-being fell upon Him, And by His scourging we are healed.
6 All of us like sheep have gone astray, Each of us has turned to his own way; But the Lord has caused the iniquity of us all To fall on Him."

In both the Old and the New Testaments Jesus is referred to as the stone that the builders rejected.

Psalms 118:22, "The stone which the builders rejected Has become the chief corner stone."

Matthew 21:42, "Jesus said to them,

**Did you never read in the Scriptures,
'The stone which the builders rejected,
This became the chief corner stone;
This came about from the Lord, And
it is marvelous in our eyes?'"**

**Mark 8:31, "And He began to teach
them that the Son of Man must suffer
many things and be rejected by the
elders and the chief priests and the
scribes, and be killed, and after three
days rise again."**

**1 Peter 2:4, "And coming to Him as to a
living stone, rejected by men, but choice
and precious in the sight of God."**

**Jesus became a curse for us so that
we could be accepted by God.**

**Galatians 3:13-14, "Christ redeemed
us from the curse of the Law, having
become a curse for us-- for it is
written, 'Cursed is everyone who
hangs on a tree'--
14 in order that in Christ Jesus the
blessing of Abraham might come to the
Gentiles, so that we might receive the
promise of the Spirit through faith."**

He, who had been in the presence of God the Father
from the beginning of eternity, felt God's total rejection.

We hear this in his anguished cry on the cross.

Matthew 27:46, "And about the ninth hour Jesus cried out with a loud voice, saying, 'Eli, Eli, lama sabachthani?' that is, 'My God, My God, why hast Thou forsaken Me?'"

This was necessary for us to have forgiveness of sins and to be able to come into a relationship with God.

Although Jesus has put to death that original root of rejection, you still have the effects of Satan's activity to confirm your rejection. You need to be healed of the pain of rejection. You need to be delivered from the "way of rejection, walking on the path of rejection."

Let's return to David. Why would David suffer from a root of rejection other than having been born of Adam? Let's consider some of the sorrows associated with rejection that Satan heaped upon David in his life.

First, consider his relationship with his father and older brothers in his earlier years. When Samuel came to anoint a new king, he told Jesse to bring all his sons before him. Jesse called 7 of his 8 sons to stand before Samuel. He did not even seem to consider presenting David to the prophet. Why would he call 7 sons but not call the eighth? Only after Samuel asked, "Don't you have any more sons?" did Jesse call for David.

1 Samuel 16:11, "And Samuel said to Jesse, Are these all the children? And he said, 'There remains

yet the youngest, and behold, he is tending the sheep.'
Then Samuel said to Jesse, Send and bring him; for
we will not sit down until he comes here."

It is interesting to note that the word used for
"youngest" [qatan] can also be translated as "the
least or unimportant." The root word [qaton] means
"to be small or insignificant." The use of this word
reflects Jesse's attitude toward David. David was
not only the "youngest" but was also considered the
most "unimportant" and "insignificant." He was not
considered important enough to be invited to the
sacrifice and to be presented before Samuel.

This attitude seems to be shared by David's oldest
brother, Eliab. Some time later when David goes to
check on 3 of his brothers who are now in Saul's
army, he gets a severe scolding from Eliab.

**1 Samuel 17:26-29, "Then David
spoke to the men who were standing
by him, saying, What will be done
for the man who kills this Philistine,
and takes away the reproach from
Israel? For who is this uncircumcised
Philistine, that he should taunt the
armies of the living God?**

**27 And the people answered him in
accord with this word, saying, 'Thus
it will be done for the man who kills
him.'**

**28 Now Eliab his oldest brother heard
when he spoke to the men; and Eliab's**

anger burned against David and he said, 'Why have you come down? And with whom have you left those few sheep in the wilderness? I know your insolence and the wickedness of your heart; for you have come down in order to see the battle.'
29 But David said, What have I done now? Was it not just a question?"

Eliab got very angry with David and accused him of having evil motives in coming to the camp. "Insolence", zadon, comes from the root word zud, meaning "to act proudly or presumptuously or rebelliously." "Wickedness" is roa, meaning "badness or evil." There is not much love or acceptance from his eldest brother.

The truth is David had come to the camp because his father commanded him to take supplies to his 3 sons in the army, take a gift to their captain, and to report back to him about the welfare of his 3 eldest. David was not acting out of rebellion but out of obedience. He did not have an evil heart but a concerned heart.

David does not seem to have been highly regarded by either his father or his oldest brother. He was the youngest. He was the most insignificant.

David found great success as the leader of Saul's army. He was given Saul's younger daughter, Michal, to marry, making him son-in-law to the king. Jonathan, Saul's son, loved David as he would have his own flesh and blood brother. But, Saul became jealous and then afraid of David's success both on and off the battlefield. As he sought to kill David, David had to flee for his life. Again, David is rejected by a father figure, the king.

I do believe David received some healing and restoration with his family while he was hiding from Saul.

1 Samuel 22:1, "So David departed from there and escaped to the cave of Adullam; and when his brothers and all his father's household heard of it, they went down there to him."

His father and brothers joined him in the cave. There was restoration in the midst of sorrow and rejection! I believe that David did receive healing for his soul. One of the final Psalms he wrote declares:

"I have been young, and now I am old; Yet I have not seen the righteous forsaken, Or his descendants begging bread" (Psalms 37:25).

Jesus told his disciples before He died on Calvary:

> **John 14:16-18, "And I will ask the Father, and He will give you another Helper, that He may be with you forever;**
> **17 that is the Spirit of truth, whom the world cannot receive, because it does not behold Him or know Him, but you know Him because He abides with you, and will be in you.**

18 "I will not leave you as orphans; I will come to you."

He promised that the Holy Spirit would always be with them.

After he died, was resurrected and before He ascended back to heaven he promised:

Matthew 28:19-20, "Go therefore and make disciples of all the nations, baptizing them in the name of the Father and the Son and the Holy Spirit,
20 teaching them to observe all that I commanded you; and lo, I am with you always, even to the end of the age."

Hebrews 13:5-6, "Let your character be free from the love of money, being content with what you have; for He Himself has said, 'I will never desert you, nor will I ever forsake you,'
6 so that we confidently say, 'The Lord is my helper, I will not be afraid. What shall man do to me?'

"I'm almost 52 years old and I still can't add." What do I mean by this? Of course I can add numbers. One plus one equals two. Numbers are easy. What is not easy is when I am seeking solutions to emotional problems. I can't always see such a simple thing as one plus one equals two.

When I was two and a half years old, my father kissed my mother and I goodbye one morning and left for work. By five o'clock that afternoon he was dead. It was even more tragic for my mother because she was seven months pregnant. I don't remember very much about this time. Every now and then I get some new insight into how it must have affected me. Children often feel rejected and forsaken/abandoned when a parent dies. They can't understand why the parent does not come back. They don't understand accidents and death. They only know their parent isn't there anymore.

When I was about five years old, my mother remarried. She married a man with four children. His wife had died giving birth to their fifth child, who also died at birth. His children were older than my brother and I. Only his two youngest children came to live with us. Suddenly I was no longer the oldest. I now had a sister who was five years older and a brother who was almost 3 years older.

My new big sister immediately bonded with my younger brother. He was her "living doll" and caring for him nurtured some maternal instinct in her. He was cute and very easy going. I was much more aggressive and mischievous. Most of my early years in our new family I felt rejected by my big sister. She just didn't care for me like she did my little brother. I never understood why.

When my mother died, my brother and I were talking to our big sister. Someone asked her, "Do you remember when your mother died?"

"Oh, yes. We were at my [maternal] grandmother's

house. We were all excited because Daddy had taken mama to the hospital to have a baby. We couldn't wait for him to come home and bring Mama and the baby. I remember standing out in the yard. As I saw the car stop in the yard I couldn't wait to see Mama and the new baby. Only Daddy got out of the car. He was crying. My grandmother ran out into the yard and saw Daddy. He must have told her what happened, but not us. All I remember is Grandmother started wailing and sobbing and fell down on an old tree stump in the yard and cried and cried. Daddy just stood there crying. I remember running from grownup to grownup begging them to tell me what was going on, begging them to tell me where Mama and the baby were. Nobody would tell me anything. I remember that day very well."

I had known my sister for forty-three years and yet not one of us had ever asked her that question. She had been carrying that sorrow around in her heart since she was ten years old. It never occurred to any of us what she had experienced.

Three years after my mother died I was sitting in a meeting worshiping the Lord and I received revelation. I knew that the death of my father had caused me to feel rejected. It was simple: One two-year-old child plus one deceased parent equaled feelings of rejection and sorrow. However, it had never occurred to me, even when my sister shared her traumatic memories that she had experienced the same loss that I had. Because I was blinded by my own self-centeredness and my own sorrow, I could not do the addition for her. Furthermore, I could not add the resulting numbers: One sister feeling rejected by the death of a parent plus one brother feeling rejected by the death of his parent equals rejection in the new relationship. I wanted people to give me grace because I had lost my father. It never occurred to me that I needed to give grace to my sister who had lost her mother. She didn't reject me because I wasn't cute like my brother. As a twelve-year-old girl, she was still suffering the rejection of her loss.

It's hard enough for us to do the simple math for the pain in our lives but extremely difficult for us to do that math in the lives of those who are close to us and may hurt us as well. We all need tutoring with our emotional math. We are all handicapped with ADS. We all need the help of the Holy Spirit. We need His healing, we need His restoration and we need His revelation.

Conclusion

In Matthew chapter ten we see Jesus gathering the 12 disciples in preparation to send them on their first mission trip without Him. He gives them the authority they need over the enemy and the power to minister as He has demonstrated for them. Then he gives them some final instructions. Two particular commands are relevant to our study.

Matthew 10:17, <u>"But beware of men; for they will deliver you up to the courts, and scourge you in their synagogues."</u>

[Underline added by author.]

Matthew 10:26-31, "Therefore do not fear them, for there is nothing covered that will not be revealed, and hidden that will not be known.
27 What I tell you in the darkness, speak in the light; and what you hear whispered in your ear, proclaim upon the housetops.
28 And do not fear those who kill the body, but are unable to kill the soul; but rather fear Him who is able to destroy both soul and body in hell.
29 Are not two sparrows sold for a cent? And yet not one of them will fall to the ground apart from your Father.
30 But the very hairs of your head are all numbered.

31 Therefore do not fear; you are of more value than many sparrows."
[Underline added by author.]

First Jesus commands them to "Beware of Men." He is warning them to be on their guard, to be cautious. Immediately following he prophesies what kinds of things men will do to them even to the point that "a man's enemies will be the members of his household." (Matthew 10:36) What Jesus says between verses 17 and 36 are enough to cause most of us to shy away from any ministry with our fellow human beings!

For this reason Jesus repeats this second command three times, "Do Not FEAR!" Actually this is the most often repeated command in the Bible. From Genesis to Revelation, in almost every book of the Bible, we are commanded about 170 times, "Do Not Be Afraid." Apparently this is one of our greatest weaknesses. Therefore, it is one of Satan's main weapons against us.

Jesus knew what was in men. He understood human nature enough to be cautious, to be alert and to warn us to beware. Even though he understood the evil nature of us all, he was not afraid to come among us and enter into intimate relationships. He felt that we, the human race, were important enough for him to abandon heaven and His exalted position with the Father and Holy Spirit, to be born in a lowly stable and live and suffer among us. People were important enough for him to die a horrible death on the cross.

Jesus is our example. If He, who knew fully what we are capable of doing to one another, was not afraid to get close to people, then we certainly have no right to seclude ourselves in fear.

We were all created in the image of God. He gave the best that He had to redeem us and bring us back into relationship with Himself. He plans for people to spend eternity with Him. Therefore, no matter how people may treat us, we must always remember how important we all are to God. What God treasures, we must treasure. What God loves, we must love. And, He loves and treasures people.

We're all just a bunch of gooney birds anyway. Aren't you glad God loves gooney birds? He made them. He loves them. So must we.

TO HIS GLORY PUBLISHING COMPANY, INC.

111 Sunnydale Court, Lawrenceville, GA 30044, U. S. A. (770) 458-7947

Order Form for Bookstores in the USA

Order Date: _____

Order Placed By: _____   By fax: _____

Address: _____   By phone: _____

City _____ ST/ZIP _____   Terms: _____

Phone#: _____

Email: _____   Discount: _____

Purchase Order#: _____

Return Policy: Within 1 Year but not before 90 days

Title and ISBN#

Price	Quantity	List Price
Shipping Method:		
Media		
UPS		
FedEx		
Other (please describe) Total Price:	Total Quantity:	

Ship To Address: Bill To Address:

TO HIS GLORY PUBLISHING COMPANY, INC. (770) 458-7947 Use Only - Billing Information

TO HIS GLORY PUBLISHING COMPANY, INC.

111 Sunnydale Court, Lawrenceville, GA 30044, U. S. A. (770) 458-7947

Order Form for Bookstores in the USA

Order Date:		
Order Placed By:		By fax:
Address:		By phone:
City	ST/ZIP	Terms:
Phone#:		
Email:		Discount:
Purchase Order#:		

Return Policy Within 1 Year but not before 90 days

Title and ISBN#

Price	Quantity	List Price
Shipping Method:		
Media		
UPS		
FedEx		
Other (please describe) Total Price:	Total Quantity:	

Ship To Address: Bill To Address:

TO HIS GLORY PUBLISHING COMPANY, INC. (770) 458-7947 Use Only - Billing Information

www.ingramcontent.com/pod-product-compliance
Lightning Source LLC
LaVergne TN
LVHW011218080426
835509LV00005B/188